D0646640

Contents

Copyright © 1980 by Publications International, Ltd.
All rights reserved
This book may not be reproduced or quoted in whole or in part by mimeograph or any other printed means or for presentation on radio or television without written permission from:

Louis Weber, President
Publications International, Ltd.
3841 West Oakton Street
Skokie, Illinois 60076

Permission is never granted for commercial purposes

Manufactured in the United States of America
1 2 3 4 5 6 7 8 9 10

BEEKMAN HOUSE
A Division of Crown Publishers, Inc.
One Park Avenue
New York, New York 10016

LIBRARY OF CONGRESS CATALOG CARD NUMBER: 80–65029
ISBN: 0–517–309947

Chief Contributing Editor: Richard M. Langworth

Contributing Editors: Jeffery I. Godshall, Walter E. Gosden, Maurice D. Hendry

Cover Design: Frank E. Peiler

Automobiles of the 1930s

If you are, as they say, "of a certain age," you'll probably remember the popular song "Brother, can you spare a dime?"—perhaps with a shudder. The Great Depression, ushered in by a plummeting New York stock market in October, 1929, was rough—*really* rough. Notwithstanding our present uncertain economic situation, we have never seen anything like it since. Let us hope we never do.

For those too young to remember, a brief recap is in order. The stock market collapse of 1929, in which 50 leading stocks fell nearly 40 points in one day, was just the opening gun. During the fourth quarter of 1929, American Telephone and Telegraph fell from 304 to 197¼ a share, General Electric from 396¼ to 169, RCA from 101 to 28. Orders for manufactured goods stopped dead. During the next two years, the net income of the 500 largest corporations in America declined 58 percent. Marginal companies expired like houseflies in the first chill of winter. Stronger companies cut back or operated part-time. Even mighty General Motors was effectively reduced to three divisions in 1933-34 through the combining of the Buick, Pontiac, and Oldsmobile sales organizations. One-third of the nation's railroads went bankrupt. Between 1928 and 1932, the national income dropped from $82 billion to $40 billion.

Even after 50 years, not all economists agree on the causes of the Great Depression. Some of the traditional reasons given are a high rate of poverty among many, too much affluence for a few, a mid 1920s recession in the farming and housing fields, and "loose money" coupled with inflation. Let's look at the facts. Personal spending amounted to 75 percent of the gross national product in 1929, compared to 64 percent in 1978. And though there were a lot of wealthy people, Federal tax cuts in 1919-21 had given everyone more take-home pay. Farm debts actually declined between 1923 and 1927; prices for livestock and crops increased in 1928-29. Residential housing investment did suffer a drop after 1927, but non-residential investment increased. The $12.1 billion peak housing investment of 1926 was almost equalled by the $10.8 billion of 1929. As for the "loose money" theory, there is little evidence of this. The money supply rose by less than four percent in 1927-28, and not at all in 1929. No price indices show any sign of inflation. The 1929 discount rate of six percent was relatively quite high. Money was not "loose."

Many theorists now believe that the market crashed and stayed weak because of the likelihood of new tariffs (Smoot-Hawley, in particular) with all they implied for international business. But whatever the cause, the results were grim. The "threadbare '30s" were hard times for all Americans.

For U.S. car makers, the crash couldn't have come at a more inopportune time. In the mid '20s, the American automobile industry had truly emerged from the horseless-carriage age. Unworkable ideas for self-propelled vehicles had been abandoned, and the internal-combustion gasoline engine (with the notable exception of the Doble steam car) reigned supreme. Engineers were engaged in wringing previously unheard of amounts of horsepower out of that engine. Designers in the great coachbuilding houses—LeBaron, Murphy, Rollston, Brewster, Waterhouse, and others—were creating some of the most extraordinary styling ever to roll on four wheels. Many new companies and makes were just getting started: Plymouth, DeSoto, Graham, Cord, Roosevelt, American Austin, Viking, Pontiac, LaSalle, Marquette. Some of the most impressive models ever built by the more established companies were just being announced.

1930 Cadillac V-16 seven-passenger sedan

In 1929 alone, for example, the number of new models was almost unbelievable. There were the front-drive Cord L-29 and Ruxton, the mighty Duesenberg Model J, the Pierce-Arrow Eights, the Auburn cabin speedster. In 1930, the multi-cylinder-engine race began with Cadillac's introduction of its fabulous Sixteen. Marmon and Peerless were also planning Sixteens, while a host of companies were readying Twelves: Packard, Lincoln, Cadillac, Auburn, Franklin, Pierce-Arrow. Stutz and Duesenberg stayed with their straight eights, but were experimenting with superchargers and four-valves-per-cylinder configurations. Ford was preparing the first low-priced V-8. Hudson was soon to release the first moderately priced "factory hot rod," the Terraplane. We were on the eve of great things in 1929. It's a shame the crash had to occur when it did, because it rendered so many wonderful ideas stillborn and put so many companies out of business.

This is the story of the Cars of the '30s, a period of high fascination for anyone who loves automobiles. The first five years of this decade are now considered the golden age of the automobile. At first, the Depression did not seriously affect the kind of people who bought Duesenbergs or Cadillacs or Packards. For a few years at least, the great cars continued—impossibly expensive, incredibly impractical, amazingly grand. The remarkable thing is that we were able to build so many of them. Britain had its Rolls-Royce and Daimler, Germany its Mercedes, Italy its Isotta Fraschini, Spain its Hispano-Suiza, and France its Deláge. But America had its Cadillac, Chrysler Imperial, Cord, Doble, Duesenberg, duPont, Franklin, LaSalle, Lincoln, Marmon, Packard, Pierce-Arrow, and Stutz. We had more grand marques and more classic cars within our own borders than all the other car-producing countries of the world combined.

Limited-production cars, of course, are only part of the story. The 1930s were years of progress for the high-volume companies, too. Innovations appeared which made the automobile a practical and reliable tool to be used, rather than a mechanical monster to be mastered. Between 1930 and 1939, we parted company with clumsy, unsynchronized manual transmissions, complicated sleeve-valve engines, ancient wood-and-fabric bodies, mechanical brakes, and solid front axles. In their place were synchromesh, semi-automatic and automatic transmissions; side-valve and overhead-valve engines; all-steel closed bodies; hydraulic brakes; and independent front suspension. The typical American car of 1930 was an upright little box on artillery-spoke wheels, with a wood-and-fabric roof. It wheezed along on four or six small cylinders, was shifted by a crotchety "crashbox," and had a suspension little different from the farm cart. Its counterpart of 1939 was a sleek "torpedo" on slotted steel wheels, with more room inside, a longer wheelbase, and a vibration-free, rubber-mounted engine. It was capable of cruising at 60, 70, or even 80 mph. By 1939, most spare tires were hidden inside the trunk, and the trunk itself was now an integral part of the body structure; radios and fresh-air heaters were options. Styling had long since departed from the square, formal lines of the '20s. After a period of streamlined depravity—typified by the Chrysler and DeSoto Airflows—smooth, flowing "organic" lines arrived. The typical 1939 car would go just as far on a tank of gas as its predecessor of the previous decade, but it would do so with more style, comfort, safety, and speed.

More than any other period in the history of the automobile, the styling and engineering progress of the 1930s determined the shape of cars as we know them today. Ever since its founding by W. C. Durant in 1908, General Motors had been striving for managerial and creative decentralization through the division concept. Ford, meanwhile, remained strongly centralized as befitted a family-owned company. GM's ultimately superior approach began to tell by the late '20s. Chevrolet first upset Ford in the production race, then moved ahead of Ford to stay. GM president Alfred E. Sloan's famous slogan, "a car for every purse and pocketbook," was the key to success. By 1939, Ford was struggling to imitate GM with its new Lincoln Zephyr and Mercury lines. But it would take at least ten more years to divisionalize Ford, and 15 years to rebuild it.

1939 Willys Model 48 four-door sedan

1936 Cord 810 convertible phaeton

Automobiles of the 1930s

Walter P. Chrysler was an old GM man, and he saw the light much earlier than Henry Ford. Although Chrysler Corporation was founded in the '20s, it really came of age in the '30s. Following a divisional structure not unlike General Motors', Walter Chrysler built the second-largest car company in the nation during the decade and the firm would remain as such until the early 1950s.

The '30s grimly thinned the ranks of the independents. By 1939, only a few of them were still in reasonably sound financial shape: Hudson, Nash, Packard, and Studebaker. Only those four—plus Crosley, which began in 1939—would survive after World War II.

A few points about the text which follows. Throughout this book you will find references to both calendar and model year production. Model year production is the actual number of any particular make or model built for a specific model year. Though most car makers in the '30s still began their model years in January, some were already shifting to fall introductions. Others built two separate series for each model year, and a few series spanned several model years. Calendar year production is simply the number of cars turned out between January 1 and December 31 of any given year. This is the figure by which the industry normally gauges a company's success. When we talk of a make's standing in the production race, or of its annual volume, we refer to calendar year production. Where specific makes and models have a particularly interesting model year figure, that total is clearly labeled as such.

Another point concerns price. All list prices are quoted in contemporary 1930s dollars, which makes them almost incomprehensible by 1980 standards. As a guide, multiply the 1930s price by five or six to get some idea of what the cars would cost new were they being made today. You may be amazed at the values offered in the '30s—or at the prices being asked for some of these cars today.

A great deal of ink has been expended on the word "classic," which has been greatly abused by wishful thinkers. Today, you can pick up any vintage-car publication and see all kinds of vehicles (even as new as 1980) described as "classics." In this book, we use the word with a special meaning and spelled with a capital "C." Briefly, Classics are those cars built between 1925-48 which are recognized as noteworthy in some way by the Classic Car Club of America (CCCA). The basis for selection involves original list price, styling, specifications, production, and other objective criteria. For reference, here are the 1930-39 American cars recognized as Classics by the CCCA:

Auburn: all except Sixes
Blackhawk
Brewster
Buick: Smith Brothers customs

Cadillac: all 1930-35; 1936-39 Series 70/72/75 Eights; all Twelves; all Sixteens; custom-bodied 60 Specials
Chrysler Imperial: 1930 Model 80; 1931-33 Series CG/CL; 1934-35 Series CW
Cord
Cunningham
Doble
Duesenberg
duPont
Franklin: all except 1933-34 Olympic Six
Graham: 1930 LeBaron or Erdmann & Rossi custom bodies
Jordon: Speedway Series Z
Kissel: 1930-31 8-126 and 8-90 White Eagle
LaSalle: 1930-33 only
Lincoln: Models L, K, KA, KB
Marmon: 1930-31 Big Eight and 88; all Sixteens
Mercer
Packard: all 1930-34; all 1935-38 except One-Twenty and Six; 1939 long-wheelbase Super Eight and Twelve
Peerless: Custom Eight
Pierce-Arrow
Reo: 1930-31 and 1933 Royale Custom Eight; 1930-31 8-35 and 8-52
Ruxton
Stearns-Knight
Stutz

For those interested in more information about the CCCA, its address is Box 443, Madison, NJ 07940. One-make clubs and their addresses, together with some remarks on the desirability and present prices of each make today, will be found in the individual chapters.

There is, of course, a certain subjective factor in judging true Classics. If you're ever in doubt about a car's qualification for that title, ask yourself: Was it built for the masses, or for the classes? Maurice D. Hendry, one of the contributors to this book, also provides a useful anecdote. Briefly and graphically, it demonstrates the intrinsic difference between the Classics and the non-Classics of the 1930s.

You are riding along to an old car meet in a friend's Model A Ford. A flicker in the rearview mirror, and you see a great nickeled radiator with creased shoulders, looming larger by the second. A monster car glides by at a mile-a-minute. You catch a glimpse of a block-long hood, distinctive disc wheels with red-splashed centers in elegantly protruding hubs, and a gorgeous interior. You can't hear anything above the tractor-chug of the Model A. But you sense that even had you been parked, you would have heard no more than a swish of tires and a silken purr from that other car's exhaust.

As it shrinks rapidly toward the horizon you shout, "What's that?" "A Packard," yells your friend.

"Is that what you mean by a Classic?" you ask. Your friend says nothing. His response is mute but eloquent: A grin. And a nod.

Auburn
Auburn Automobile Company
Auburn, Indiana

The Auburns best remembered by enthusiasts today are those produced in the late 1920s and in the '30s, but the firm has a history which dates back to 1903. In that year, two Indiana carriage builders, Frank and Morris Eckhart, launched a chain-drive single-cylinder runabout which sold for $800. Two-, four-, and six-cylinder cars followed successively in the years through 1912. A notable Auburn introduced in 1919 was the Beauty Six, which had a streamlined body, disc wheels, step plates instead of running boards, and windshield wings—all very advanced for the time.

The Auburn of those years was never in great demand. It was a good car, but the Eckharts lacked an effective sales organization. After the First World War, a recession cut into automobile sales and Auburn produced fewer than 4000 cars a year from 1919 to 1922.

The company's low-key image changed abruptly in 1924 with the arrival of Erret Lobban Cord. The 30-year-old Cord was variously described as a "boy wonder" and a "profane, bespectacled capitalist." His claim to fame was salesmanship. Five years earlier, Cord had started as a salesman for Moon cars, and quickly worked his way up to become general manager, and then director, of the Chicago company. In the process, he had piled up around $100,000. His reputation preceded him to Auburn, where he was asked to step in as general manager. After he sold 750 leftover Auburns, which netted the company enough cash to pay off its debts, Cord was made a vice-president. By 1926, he had become president and chief stockholder of the Auburn Automobile Company.

Under Cord's guidance, Auburn prospered in the 1920s. Its most notable cars of that decade were its new Eights, the 8-88 and 8-115 (with 88 and 115 bhp, respectively). Auburn gained a modest competition image, hugely increased its export operations, upgraded its dealer network, and passed the 20,000 mark in annual production by 1929. Auburns of the late '20s and early '30s were fast, good-looking and reliable, yet incredibly low priced. Eights sold for as little as $1395, Sixes for as little as $995. Though Eights were more vivid performers than the Sixes, all Auburns were appreciated for their high style and solid quality.

After 1930, E. L. Cord dropped the Six to concentrate on the Eights and ultimately, a Twelve. The 1930 6-85 six-cylinder series consisted of only three models—cabriolet, sedan, and sport sedan—priced from $995 to $1095. The engine was built by Lycoming, a Pennsylvania Company purchased by Cord in 1929. This was a sturdy unit of 185 cubic inches and produced 70 horsepower at 3400 rpm. Despite its modest price, the Six was by no means a dull car. It rode a 120-inch wheelbase, and was a smooth, clean-looking design. Nevertheless, Auburn sales dropped by almost 50 percent in 1930, and the continuing Depression convinced management that a Six was not profitable enough to continue for 1931.

The 1930 Auburn Eights came in two series. The lower-price line, the 8-95, had a 125-inch wheelbase and was an unquestionable bargain. The 8-95 engine had the 6-85's bore and stroke, but with two extra cylinders its displacement went up to 247 cubic inches. Price range of the 8-95 was $1195-$1295 and the series duplicated the Six's body styles, except that a five-passenger phaeton sedan was also offered.

Further up the price scale, in the same four body styles as the 8-95, was the 8-125 series. Its larger Lycoming eight displaced 298.6 cubic inches and developed 125 bhp at 3600 rpm. Though most 125s tipped the scales at around 3900 pounds, they were capable of close to 90 mph, an astonishing speed in 1930. The year before, this same engine in a 3000-pound speedster body had powered Auburn's first 100-mph automobile.

Auburn was one of the first car companies to record increased sales after the 1929 stock market crash. Production zoomed to a record 32,301 units in 1931 and was the result of a dealer expansion program, plus the all-eight-cylinder line of beautiful, fleet, luxurious, and bargain-priced models.

1930 Auburn 8-95 phaeton sedan

1930 Auburn 8-125 two-passenger cabriolet

Auburn

The 1931 lineup reflected E. L. Cord's cagey sales strategy. Auburn now lopped off its slower selling models—the small Six and the big Eight—and bored out its smaller eight-cylinder engine to 268.6 cid which boosted output to 98 bhp. Larger, more rakish bodies were placed on a longer 127-inch wheelbase and two series, Standard and Custom, were offered. Customs were equipped with a free-wheeling transmission. Speedsters, coupes, cabriolets, broughams, phaeton sedans, and sedans were available, as well as a seven-passenger sedan built on a special 136-inch wheelbase. Miraculously, Auburn was able to sell these cars for as little as $945 (Standard) or $1145 (Custom). As *Business Week* commented at the time, "it was more car for the money than the public had ever seen."

Although the 1931 Auburn Eight was a remarkable buy, the 1932 Auburn Twelve was even more incredible. It was the least expensive V-12 ever produced: $975 for the Standard coupe, $1275 for the top-of-the-line Custom Speedster. Its Lycoming engine was built to the design of Auburn chief engineer George Kublin, and displaced 391 cubic inches with a healthy 160 bhp at 3500 rpm. The double-braced frame spanned a 133-inch wheelbase. Custom Twelves featured a Columbia dual-ratio rear axle with a choice of 4.55:1 or 3.04:1 ratios and which could be switched at speeds under 40 mph, effectively providing the car with six forward speeds. The Eights continued as before. All Auburns were available in the usual six body styles, plus long-wheelbase sedans in the eight-cylinder series. The beautiful V-12 boattail speedsters, so rare today, were magnificent expressions of Auburn styling in 1932.

Despite what appeared to be a peerless line of cars, Auburn sales plunged in 1932. Production for the year was only 7939. In 1933, it dropped to 4636, and in 1934,

1931 Auburn 8-100 Custom four-door sedan

1933 Auburn V-12 Custom sedan

it was 4703. Why this happened mystified E. L. Cord, though with hindsight the reason is clear: A V-12 at any price simply didn't interest buyers in the depths of the Depression. Nor, for that matter, did Auburn's Eight, which had exhausted what market it had in 1931. Both cars had a reputation for size and performance that made people equate them, perhaps, with more expensive makes. By this time, Cord himself was spread too thin building his far-flung business empire. He'd already bought Duesenberg in 1929, and had built a front-wheel-drive car bearing his own name the same year.

1932 Auburn 8-100 two-passenger cabriolet

1934 Auburn 850 two-passenger cabriolet

1935 Auburn phaeton with Cummins Diesel engine

Later, he had purchased the Lycoming and Ansted engine companies, several midwestern industrial corporations, and Checker Cab, as well as holding shipbuilding and aviation interests. Perhaps in order to avoid a scandal over the management of his enterprises, Cord went to England in 1934 where he dropped out of sight. The fortunes of his company were eventually handed over to Harold T. Ames, president of Duesenberg.

The model lineup for 1933-34 comprised Eights and Twelves, as in 1932, but also saw a revival of the Six, designated the 652. Its Lycoming engine displaced 210

1936 Auburn 852 Supercharged sedan

cubic inches and offered 85 bhp at 3500 rpm. This car was priced as low as $695, and was offered in Standard or Custom trim on a 119-inch wheelbase. It didn't sell. A controversial 1934 facelift, which introduced radical streamlining features including a shovel-nose grille, is often tagged with the blame, but 1934 was not a good sales year for any make.

When Harold T. Ames arrived from Duesenberg, he brought with him Gordon Miller Buehrig and August Duesenberg. Buehrig was given a modest $50,000 budget and told to do what he could to upgrade Auburn styling for 1935. Duesenberg was handed the 1935 eight-cylinder engine assignment, in conjunction with Schwitzer-Cummins and Lycoming. The result was a pretty line of '35 models including the legendary 851 Speedster—Auburn's final glory.

Buehrig didn't have enough money to fully redesign the '35s, so he worked with leftover '34 Twelves. To create the '35 Speedster he restyled the body of the Twelve Speedster from the cowl forward with a new radiator, a sleek hood, beautifully curved pontoon fenders, and exterior exhausts. Duesenberg, meanwhile, created a new engine. To save on tooling costs, this unit was basically an extension of the 1934 six with the same bore and stroke, but two more cylinders, of course. The end product displaced 279.2 cubic inches and developed 115 bhp, or 150 bhp with a Schwitzer-Cummins supercharger. Speedster models came only with the supercharger, would hit 100 mph right off the showroom floor, and were among the most breathtakingly beautiful automobiles of all time. Yet, their base price was just $2245. Again, Auburn offered a tremendous bargain for the money.

The 1936 line was a repeat of 1935, the Sixes receiving the '654' designation and the Eights becoming the '852'. Despite what could only be termed a brilliant line of cars—cabriolets, broughams, phaetons, and sedans as well as the 852 Speedster—production continued to plummet. Total output in 1934 had been only 5163; in 1936 it was just 1848. Speedster production for both years totaled around 600. In 1936, E. L. Cord returned from England to salvage his empire, but he found the Securities and Exchange Commission and the IRS waiting to launch major investigations of his doings. A promised 1937 Auburn never materialized.

Cord managed to keep most of his fortune and was involved in western land speculation in his later years. He is not remembered with reverence in Auburn circles, but it is doubtful that the marque would have evolved into what it did without him. Under both E. L. Cord and Harold Ames, Auburn wrote some of motoring's great history in the 1930s.

Auburn owners wishing to get in touch with fellow enthusiasts may write to the Auburn-Cord-Duesenberg Club, P.O. Box 217, Skippack, Pennsylvania 19474.

photo credits: *Henry Ford Museum; Motor Vehicle Manufacturers Association*

American Austin

American Austin Car Company, Inc.
Butler, Pennsylvania

When Sir Herbert Austin, the well-known English manufacturer of cars bearing his name, came to America in 1929, he had many people excited over his plan to build cars in the U.S.A. After a tour of the country, he announced that the American Austin would be built in Butler, Pennsylvania. Detroit shook its collective head, but Butler wasn't such a strange choice. It had access to industrial services, an eager work force, and it was close enough to east coast ports to make importing components from England quite feasible. The basic concept of the car itself seemed promising, too. When production started in Butler during May, 1930, the company claimed it had close to 200,000 orders for the new ultra-light, ultra-economical car.

Austins were built from 1930 through 1934, using the same engine throughout the production run. This was an L-head four which displaced 46 cubic inches, had only two main bearings, and developed 13 or 14 brake horsepower at 3200 rpm. A roadster and coupe were offered in 1930, priced at $445 and $465, respectively. In 1931, a business coupe, Deluxe coupe, and 2-4 passenger cabriolet were added. Once production fired up, some of these prices were cut. The 1931 Austin roadster cost only $395 and the elaborate cabriolet just $550. Prices were reduced again in 1933 in an effort to boost sales: The business coupe dropped to $275 and the roadster to $315.

For awhile Austin's prospects looked good—but only for awhile—and the 1930 production total of 8558 units was never exceeded. Figures were 1279 cars for 1931, 3846 for 1932, 4726 for 1933, and an estimated 1300 for 1934. Two factors were largely responsible for Austin's demise: One was the general business decline of the Depression years; the other was the fact that even in bad times, Americans didn't take to midget cars. To be sure, the American Austin was a midget. Its wheelbase, at 75 inches, was fully 16 inches less than a VW Beetle's. Also, the Austin weighed only 1100-1200 pounds, and Americans were notoriously leary about light cars in those years, as they would be for a few decades more. The Austin was an attractive little car, designed in part by Alexis de Sakhnoffsky, but this didn't seem to matter. In 1935, production ground to a halt.

Austins provided a touch of amusement in a drab period for America and for a few people, they became a sort of reverse status symbol, much like the Beetle would be in the 1950s. Al Jolson, who loved cars and usually drove Packards or Lincolns, bought the first Austin coupe delivered to a private buyer. He was followed by numerous other Hollywood stars—Buster Keaton, Slim Summerville, and the "Our Gang" kiddies. Austins even starred in a movie. They were used as "steeds" for a knightly battle in Will Rogers' "A Connecticut Yankee in King Arthur's Court." It was a great scene—but it didn't help to sell Austins.

Keeping alive the memory of this little car is the Pacific Bantam Austin Club, 4636 Midsite Avenue, Covina, California 91722.

photo credit: *Motor Vehicle Manufacturers Association*

1930 American Austin two-door Deluxe coupe

American Bantam

American Bantam Car Co.
Butler, Pennsylvania

Energetic Roy S. Evans offered to buy the down-and-out American Austin factory in 1935, but he faced some formidable obstacles. The company owed $75,000 in back taxes and interest, and Pullman Standard had a mortgage on the property for $150,000. However, the Federal court with jurisdiction over the bankrupt firm felt Evans might salvage the situation and awarded him the factory for $5000 cash—only 1/2000ths of its appraised valuation. Evans secured a $250 million loan from the Reconstruction Finance Corporation, and hired talent to help him create a new car.

Styling for the revised model, called the American Bantam, was assigned to Alexis de Sakhnoffsky, who had created the original American Austin. For the Bantam, de Sakhnoffsky styled a new front end featuring a smooth hood and a rounded grille and also redesigned the fenders and rear deck. His bill came to only $300, and Evans retooled the entire line for a mere $7000.

Racing engineer Harry Miller was hired to work on the mechanical changes, but his efforts were confined to a redesigned manifold. Butler's own engineers contributed most of the engine alterations. They replaced the Austin's expensive roller bearings with Babitt bearings, added full-pressure lubrication, a new three-speed transmission, Hotchkiss final drive, and Ross cam-and-lever steering. Engine displacement was unchanged, though three main bearings were used instead of two after 1939. The wheelbase remained at 75 inches, as on the Austin, but the wheel size shrank from 18 to 16 inches in 1937, and to 15 inches in 1938. The frame and cross-members of the Bantam were heavier than the Austin's.

For 1937, two roadsters and three coupes were offered, priced at $381-$492. For 1938 and 1939, several new models appeared, including a speedster with a pretty "Duesenberg sweep" side panel, and the novel Boulevard Delivery. The latter had an open driver's compartment ahead of a squared-off panel body. It was described as "a jewel box on wheels," and although it was certainly unique, it didn't sell well.

The 1938 Bantam line included three roadsters, four coupes, and a station wagon as well as the speedster and Boulevard Delivery. For 1939, a convertible called the Riveria was added. Designed by Alex Tremulis, it sold for about $500. Tremulis has recalled that the Riveria would cruise at 75-80 mph and average 42.5 mpg (presumably at considerably lower speeds).

Bantam production continued into 1941, but even dynamic Roy Evans wasn't able to convince Americans of the value of his tiny package. Bantam output was about 2000 cars in 1938 and 1200 in 1939. For 1940-41, production failed to reach 1000 units and ceased altogether shortly after the 1941 model year began. Bantam then concentrated on building a prototype for what ultimately became the Army Jeep, which it also manufactured during WW II. Though Bantam didn't build as many Jeeps as Ford and Willys-Overland, it does get credit for designing the original.

The unique little Bantam is covered by the Pacific Bantam Austin Club, 4636 Midsite Avenue, Covina, California 91722.

photo credit: *Motor Vehicle Manufacturers Association*

1938 American Bantam "60" four-passenger speedster

Buick & Marquette

Buick Division, General Motors Corporation, Flint, Michigan

David Dunbar Buick was a canny Scottish industrialist who saw an opportunity to profit from the horseless carriage phenomenon. He built his first Buick in 1903, a car using a flat-twin engine and chain drive. One of its significant features was overhead valves—very rare then, but a feature of all Buick automobiles ever since. The Buick company became one of the original members of General Motors, which was founded in 1908 by W. C. Durant. Six-cylinder engines first appeared in 1914, and were the only type used in Buicks from 1925 to 1930. By then, Buick's market had been established as comprising mostly upper-class and professional people who had moved up from a Chevrolet, Oakland or Oldsmobile. Even though the Depression cut out much of this market, the company quickly

1930 Marquette Model 35 five-passenger phaeton

1930 Buick Series 60 limousine

1931 Buick Series 50 convertible coupe

recovered during the later '30s, and was fourth in production volume by 1938.

The six-cylinder line for 1930 consisted of two engines: 257.5 cubic inches with 80.5 horsepower for the Series 40; 331.3 cid with 99 bhp for the Series 50 and 60. Wheelbases were 118, 124, and 132 inches for the 40, 50 and 60, respectively and prices averaged around $1300, $1500, and $1700 for the three models. Styling was conservative and marked by a large barrel-shaped radiator.

Buick's ill-fated junior make, the Marquette, was introduced in 1929 and expired after 1930. Marquette was part of a plan to give Buick and GM broader market coverage in line with the general proliferation of nameplates that had begun in the mid '20s. In 1926, Oakland introduced the Pontiac; in 1927, Cadillac spawned LaSalle. Oldsmobile's Viking, like the Marquette, was introduced in early 1929. While Pontiac eventually eclipsed Oakland and the LaSalle sold well for awhile, both the Viking and Marquette were failures. Buick sold only 28,000 Marquettes in the U.S. for both 1929 and 1930, although another 7000 were sold in Canada and other export markets.

The Marquette departed from normal Buick practice by having an L-head, instead of an overhead valve, engine (although Buick had built an L-head truck engine in 1913). Actually, Marquette's engine was Oldsmobile-based: It displaced 213 cubic inches and produced 67.5 bhp. The 1930 edition listed at about $1000 and came in six body styles: two- and four-door sedans, sport and business coupes, touring car, and roadster. Marquette production was 15,490 for 1929 and 12,331 for 1930. A few leftovers were registered in 1931. Overall, the division sold about one Marquette for every ten Buicks.

The decisions to move up the price scale and to adopt eight-cylinder engines were made before the Wall Street crash, so Buick's sales problems in the early 1930s were the result of bad timing. Certainly there was little to fault about the 1931 models. The five-main-bearing eight-cylinder engines, developed by chief engineer F. A. Bower, were among the most advanced of their day—smooth, and reliable. There were three in all. The Series 40 unit displaced 220.7 cid and had 77 bhp; for the Series 60 this was increased to 272.6 cubic inches and 90 bhp; the Series 80 and 90 powerplants displaced 344.8 cubic inches and offered 104 bhp. A very lengthy model lineup of sedans, coupes, phaetons, convertibles, roadsters, and a Series 90 limousine was offered. The Buick 40 for 1931 used the 114-inch wheelbase formerly applied to the Marquette, while wheelbases of the 50, 60, and 80/90 were 118, 124 and 132 inches, respectively. In various forms, these new straight eights would serve as the basis of Buick powerplants for the next 22 years.

The company proved the mettle of its new engines at the 1931 Indianapolis 500, when a Buick-powered racer driven by Phil Shafer qualified at 105.1 mph and averaged 86.3 mph for the Indiana classic. Even off the showroom floor, the '31s were quick: 10-60 mph came up in about 25 seconds and a top speed of 90 mph was attainable.

In 1932, all Buicks were improved by the introduction of "Silent Second Syncro-Mesh" transmission; horsepower rose to 82.5, 95, and 113 on the three engines. Horsepower and wheelbase lengths continued to increase in 1933, but Buick sales did not. Calendar year production, which had been over 100,000 since 1922, plunged to 88,000 units in 1931, then to 42,000 in 1932, and 41,000 in 1933.

In October, 1933, Harlow H. Curtice was appointed Buick's president and the fortunes of the division changed almost immediately. Curtice's goal was "more speed for less money." His first move toward that end was the all-new 117-inch wheelbase Series 40 of 1934 with a new 233-cid eight producing 93 bhp, and priced at less than $1000.

Another factor behind Buick's sales upturn in 1934 was styling. For the first time, Buick was a smooth, streamlined car instead of a boxy throwback to the "Roaring '20s." The Series 40 masterfully blended an inexpensive-to-produce Chevrolet-size body with massive Buick styling. Like all Buicks it featured GM's new "Knee-Action" independent front suspension. The Series 40 skipped the flashy soft top models in favor of the more popular coupes and sedans which helped Buick production rise to 78,000 units for 1934. For cal-

1934 Buick Series 40 four-door sedan

endar 1935, Buick was back over the 100,000 mark; by 1939 it had topped 230,000 cars, an all-time record.

Also in 1934, Curtice launched a $64 million factory modernization program, which was not fully completed until 1940. Ploughing back 1934 receipts into modernization of the Flint plant left little money available to alter the 1935 models, so the same offerings were fielded for another year. This consisted of the Series 40, 50, 60, and 90, with straight eights displacing 233, 235, 278, and 344 cubic inches, respectively. The Series 40, however, added a convertible coupe to its offerings.

More extensive changes were made in 1936. Buicks now received GM's all-steel "Turret Top" bodies introduced that year. Engines had aluminum pistons and more horsepower. Revised styling was accompanied by four new model designations which are still familiar

1932 Buick Series 90 limousine

1934 Buick Series 60 convertible coupe

1933 Buick Series 60 victoria coupe

1935 Buick Series 60 club sedan

Buick & Marquette

today: the Special (Series 40), Century (60), Roadmaster (80), and Limited (90). In 1940, these would be joined by the Series 50 Super, another model name that would continue through the 1950s.

Buick styling for 1936 directly influenced the company's revival that year. The new design was the work of Harley Earl, head of GM's Art & Colour Studio—the first formal styling department ever organized in a major car company. Earl liked streamlining, and the '36 Buick got it. The cars were more rounded than ever; windshields were swept back at a greater angle; and the trunk became an integral part of the body instead of a separate, detachable fixture. The die-cast grille was a massive, rounded affair with vertical bars. The public loved the whole package and bought over 200,000 Buicks that year. Calendar 1936 production was close to 180,000 units and Buick fortunes returned to their pre-Depression height.

Important, too, in 1936 was a new 120-bhp eight which displaced 320 cubic inches. This engine powered

1936 Buick Limited limousine

1936 Buick Special business coupe

1936 Buick Century sedan

all models except the Series 40 Special, which retained its 233-cid, 93-bhp engine. The 320-cid eight offered its most interesting performance when installed in the Century. Since the Century weighed only around 3700 pounds, compared to as much as 4600 pounds for the Limited, it was an incredibly fast car. The 320 engine gave the Century genuine 100-mph cruising capability and 10-60 mph acceleration in the 18-19 second range. The sedan sold for as little as $1035; the rakish convertible cost only $1135. The Century gained a reputation as a factory-built hot rod built for anyone with $1000 in his pocket who liked to be faster off the line than anybody else in his price class.

After the styling, engineering, and production triumphs of 1936, there seemed no need for drastic change in 1937. Harley Earl wasn't quite satisfied, however, so the Buick line was accordingly facelifted. Earl used the basic 1936 Turret Top body, but applied elongated fenders with blunt trailing edges. The grille adopted horizontal bars and the side hood vents were of complementary design. Buick was probably the best-looking GM car for 1937, a styling leader for the entire industry.

While the 1937 Century, Roadmaster, and Limited retained their 320-cid engine unchanged, the Special's engine was increased to 248 cid by a stroke increase and now developed about 100 bhp. Factory test figures showed that a Special would go from 10 to 60 mph in 19.2 seconds. This was fine performance and only a second slower than the hot Century. All 1937 Buicks were equipped with several new features: hypoid rear axle, improved generators, running-board-mounted radio antennas, defrosters, and front and rear anti-sway bars. Buick claimed an industry first this year by introducing the steering wheel horn ring.

Buick Limiteds, beginning with the 1936 model, were rather special cars, which have generally been overlooked by today's enthusiasts. All were of the "trunk-back" style, with a faired-in luggage compartment and dual spare tires nestled in long, pontoon fenders. A formal sedan of elegant proportions was offered for 1936-37 and featured a glass partition between the front and rear compartments along with luxurious trim. Though only 233 formals were built in 1936 and 1937, they were the "class" of the line, and sold for less than $2300. The Limited Series included six- and eight-passenger sedans and a limousine from 1936 through 1939. Limited chassis were also supplied in quantity to body builders such as Eureka, Miller, Sayers & Scoville, and Flxible, for hearse, ambulance, and flower-car applications.

Earl made few styling changes for the 1938 Buicks, which were distinguished mainly by a new grille composed of fewer, thicker horizontal bars. Under the skin, however, were extensive alterations that made a good car even better. The suspension of all Buicks now had coil springs at each corner—another first for the industry. This resulted in a major ride improvement, especially in conjunction with shock absorbers that were four times the size of those used on most other cars of the period. The 1938 engines were dubbed "Dynaflash"

1937 Buick Limited six-passenger sedan

1938 Buick Century two-door touring sedan

and were unchanged in displacement from their predecessors. However, thanks to new domed high-compression pistons, horsepower went up to 107 bhp for the Specials and 141 bhp for the Century, Roadmaster, and Limited. Offered on Specials only was a five-speed semi-automatic transmission, which developed a poor service record and was abandoned after 1938. Buick did not attempt another clutchless drive until the Dynaflow transmission appeared ten years later.

Buick closed out the 1930s with a lower, mildly facelifted 1939 range, featuring a waterfall-type grille, "streamboards" (optional closed-in running boards), and a sunroof option on some models. Sidemount spare tires were available, though they were not ordered as often as in the past. The Special, which had grown to a 122-inch wheelbase by 1938, was shortened for a 120-inch wheelbase chassis. Century, Roadmaster and Limited retained their 1938 wheelbases of 126, 133, and 140 inches, respectively. Body style offerings were extensive and prices were still moderate: You could pay as little as $894 for a Special business coupe, or as much as $2453 for a Limited limousine. The rakish Century convertible sport phaeton sold for $1713, and the Century sport coupe was priced at just $1175. Rumble seats

were dropped for 1939 convertible models, while Buick introduced another innovation, flashing turn signals, which were installed at the rear only where they were part of the trunk emblem. Also in 1939, Buick went to a column-mounted gearshift and adopted refillable shock absorbers. Though the waterfall grille was a questionable styling feature, the '39s retained the individuality and generally clean design of the '38s. Styling and engineering had steadily improved throughout the decade, rewarding Buick Division with strong public approval.

Collectors of Buick cars tend to favor the pre-1934 models and the post-1937s. The 1938 model is particularly favored, especially the Century and low-production Limited. There's a strong distinction made by enthusiasts between 1937 and 1938: The same model and body style may be relatively undesirable in 1937 guise, but could be a red hot collector's item as a 1938.

The 4000-member Buick Club of America welcomes these outstanding cars of the '30s. Its address is Box 853, Garden Grove, California 92642.

---

photo credits: *Buick Motor Division, General Motors Corp.*

1938 Buick Roadmaster convertible phaeton

Cadillac & LaSalle

Cadillac Division of GM, Detroit, Michigan

Regardless of its cars, Cadillac would have perished in the Depression had it been an independent. Calendar year production, which (including LaSalle) reached an unprecedented 41,000 units in 1928, plunged after the 1929 stock market crash. Cadillac Division, like other manufacturers of prestige models, found itself with a line of superb cars which no one wanted—or wanted to be seen in. Though many more people remained solvent in the Depression than is commonly thought, most preferred to drive around in Fords rather than flaunt any wealth they had conserved.

Ironically, the Depression sounded the death knell for Cadillac's arch rival Packard, despite that firm's own valiant efforts to survive. While Cadillac could continue to build ultra-luxurious cars in small quantities with the financial backing of GM, Packard, as an independent, had to change course or die. Packard temporarily survived by introducing the middle-priced One-Twenty and One-Ten series, but in so doing, abandoned its blue-chip image. Packard thus began losing its traditional wealthy clientele so that even before World War II, Cadillac production had overhauled Packard's in the high-dollar segment of the market.

Perils of the Depression aside, Cadillac Division entered 1930 with a splendid array of cars. The new line leader that year was the magnificent V-16 with an overhead-valve, 452-cid engine producing 165 bhp and 320 pounds-feet of torque. This was one of the great cars of its era. It was available, theoretically, in 33 different models, sub-models or trim variations, and ranged in price from $5350 for a two-passenger roadster to $8750 for a town cabriolet. The V-16 could cruise at 70 mph, return about eight miles to a 15-cent gallon of gas, and get 150 miles to a quart of oil.

Though a Cadillac Sixteen could do 90 mph, brute performance was not its forte. Rather, it was designed to suit the luxury-car buyer of the age with smooth, effortless power and a minimum of gearshifting. Cadillac called Sixteen power "a continuous flow . . . constantly at full-volume efficiency . . . flexible . . . instantly responsive."

The Sixteen had only been on the market nine months when the Division introduced yet another multi-cylinder giant, the Cadillac Twelve. The Twelve's engine was basically that of the Sixteen with four fewer cylinders. It displaced 370 cubic inches for an output of 135 horsepower and 284 pounds-feet of torque. The Twelve bodies were not as large as Sixteens. The latter were mounted on an enormous 148-inch wheelbase, while the V-12 fit easily on the 140-inch-wheelbase chassis used for the eight-cylinder models. Though the Twelve was not as fast as the Sixteen, its engine was free-revving and had a reputation for smooth, even power. Top speed of the V-12 roadster was about 85 mph with the standard rear axle ratio, and the car would cruise all day at 70 mph. The Twelve was also considerably cheaper than the Sixteen: Its 11 body styles ranged in price from $3795 to $4895.

Despite their unquestioned performance and majestic appearance, the multi-cylinder Cadillacs failed to

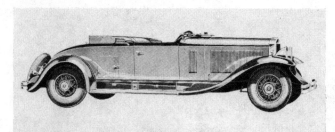

1930 Cadillac V-8 two-passenger roadster

1930 Cadillac V-8 five-passenger coupe

1930 Cadillac V-8 five-passenger sedan

1930 Cadillac V-8 town sedan

1931 Cadillac V-8 Fleetwood all-weather phaeton

1931 Cadillac V-8 Fleetwood roadster

sell. The Division built 3250 Sixteens and 5725 Twelves for the combined 1930-31 model years, the best figure ever recorded. Model year production was fair in 1932, but from 1933 on, Cadillac never built more than 1000 Twelves and 300 Sixteens annually.

In 1938, both overhead-valve multi-cylinder engines were dropped, but Cadillac had one more try with an L-head V-16. At 431 cubic inches and 185 horsepower, the new engine was smaller, lighter, and yet more powerful than its ohv predecessor. Model year output was 311 in 1938, 136 in 1939, and 61 in 1940, the final year.

There were two reasons for the failure of these top-of-the-line Cadillacs. In the early '30s, staggeringly expensive cars with more than eight cylinders seemed socially inappropriate to many people. After an initial sales burst, cars like these were avoided by customers in preference to the cheaper, less ostentatious, but by no means inferior, Cadillac Eights. Later on, the big engines were outmoded by advancing technology. The introduction of precision-insert connecting rod bearings helped eliminate knock and high-speed wear in smaller engines with fewer than 12 cylinders so there was little reason for choosing a Twelve or a Sixteen over an Eight.

By contrast, the Cadillac Eights were fairly consistent sellers throughout the decade. Model year production hung around 10,000 units in 1930 and 1931; after dipping briefly to the 2000-3000 level in 1932-33, output increased rapidly. With the introduction of the low-priced V-8 Series 60 in 1936, production again surged past 10,000 units, and by 1939 it was up to over 13,000 cars. These steady sales were due to Cadillac's reliable cast-iron L-head V-8s and a line of competitively-priced models offered in a wide range of body styles.

The Cadillac V-8 of the early '30s was based on a 341-cid engine introduced in 1928. During 1930-35, this engine displaced 353 cubic inches and produced from 95 to 130 bhp. The new, completely redesigned L-heads of 1936 were smaller and lighter, yet equally powerful. A 346-cid 90-degree V-8 with 135 bhp was the basis of most Cadillac V-8s from that year on. (The Series 60 had a 322-cid engine in 1936, but from 1937 on it, too, used the 346.) This respected powerplant remained in production until Cadillac launched its new ohv short-stroke V-8 in 1949. Though it had its limits, the 346 was capable of excellent performance and reasonable economy. It would propel the lighter 1938-39 Cadillacs to nearly 100 mph, with 0-60 mph acceleration times of

1932 Cadillac V-12 seven-passenger sedan

1932 Cadillac V-8 two-passenger coupe

1932 Cadillac V-8 five-passenger all-weather phaeton

1932 Cadillac V-8 Fleetwood roadster

Cadillac & LaSalle

15-16 seconds—performance that was no mean feat for 4500-pound luxury cars in the years before the war.

Unlike many of its luxury-class rivals, most Cadillac bodies were designed and built in-house, either by Fisher or Fleetwood. Few chassis were sent out to independent custom body builders. This enabled designers like Harley Earl to maintain a consistent Cadillac look in the styling of the whole car instead of just the radiator and hood shape. The years 1930-31 were the golden age for Cadillac coachwork: Opulent, thick-collared vertical radiators announced a beautifully rounded hood and clean, flowing body lines. Body styles were numerous. The 1930 Fisher-bodied Eight spanned seven models priced from $3300 to $4000: two coupes, three sedans, a convertible, and an Imperial limousine. Fleetwood Customs numbered no less than 14 models, including a roadster, sedanette, phaetons, two cabriolets, and a limousine brougham. Fleetwood prices aver-

aged between $3450 for the two-passenger roadster to $5145 for the town cabriolet or limousine. The most elegant body of this period was the Madame X, distinguished by its slender, chrome-edged door and windshield moldings.

Square-rigged styling began to dissolve with the advent of the more rounded 1932 models, but 1933 marked the big transition from the classic shape to streamlined forms. While the 1933 models retained the basic 1932 body, Harley Earl developed new styling features such as skirted fenders, Vee'd radiators, and rakish windshields. A significant improvement introduced on the '33s was the first Cadillac vent wing window, called "No-Draft Ventilation." These cars are prized by many today as the epitome of early and late classic-era design.

Styling for 1934, now fully revised, was prefigured by Cadillac's exotic Chicago World's Fair show car of 1933. For this custom-bodied special and the 1934 production models, Earl moved away from formal upright forms into the realm of pontoon fenders, slant-back radiator grilles, torpedo-style headlights, and rakish rear decks. He even tried a novel two-piece bumper design, probably

1933 Cadillac V-8 Fleetwood seven-passenger sedan

1933 Cadillac V-8 roadster

1934 Cadillac V-8 convertible sedan

1934 Cadillac V-8 convertible coupe

1935 Cadillac V-8 two-passenger coupe

1935 Cadillac V-8 seven-passenger sedan

inspired by the wings of the biplane, but it was unpopular as it was clumsy-looking and was abandoned in 1935. The years 1935-36 saw relatively dumpy Cadillac styling: Roundness prevailed over squareness and even the windows were potato-shaped.

Everything changed again in 1938, when young (William L.) Bill Mitchell, an Earl protegé, conjured up the Sixty Special as an addition to the Series 60 V-8 line which had been successfully introduced in 1936. The three regular 60 series models—coupe, sedan and convertible—were priced at around $1700, or about $600 cheaper than their least-expensive predecessors. Mitchell's crisp and elegant 60 Special for 1938 added dramatic styling to the 60's sound engineering and decent performance. The car was very square, with chrome-edged side windows and flat-backed pontoon fenders. It was compact for a Cadillac and is considered to be one of the most beautiful cars of all time. At $2020, it was a bargain.

In 1939, Cadillac promoted its wide variety of Eights, and ended the year with an output 10,000 units higher than 1938. Styling was a mild facelift of the previous year's car. The 346 engine was unchanged, and Cadillac had now blanketed the V-8 luxury market with its Fisher and Fleetwood models. The Series 61 rode a 126-inch wheelbase and offered coupe, sedan, convertible, and convertible sedan models priced from $1610 to $2170. The 60 Special sedan was a distinct model on its own 127-inch wheelbase priced at $2090. The Series 75 comprised the usual plethora of Fleetwood bodies on a long 141-inch wheelbase with prices that ranged from $2995 (sedan) to $5115 (limousine).

The 1930s were years of technological progress at Cadillac. The division had introduced clashless Syncro-Mesh transmission in 1929, and in 1932 offered "Triple-Silent" Syncro-Mesh with helical gears for all three forward speeds. No-draft ventilation and vacuum-assisted brakes followed in 1933; independent front suspension bowed in 1934; all-steel "Turret Top" bodies debuted in 1935; hydraulic brakes were offered on all models except Sixteens for 1936; the first of what would become Cadillac's traditional egg-crate grilles was seen in 1937; and, column gearshift and optional turn signals were featured for 1938.

The decade also witnessed the rise and fall of Cadillac's junior edition, the LaSalle. Though LaSalle was

1936 Cadillac V-8 Fleetwood convertible sedan

1936 Cadillac Series 60 convertible coupe

1937 Cadillac Series 75 convertible sedan

1938 Cadillac Series 75 convertible coupe

1939 Cadillac Sixty Special touring sedan

1933 LaSalle V-8 town sedan

Cadillac & LaSalle

actually born in 1927 and died in 1940, its fate was sealed during the '30s.

LaSalle had first appeared on a wheelbase smaller than Cadillac's and had accounted for one-quarter of division sales. In 1929, LaSalle outproduced Cadillac 11 to 9. The 1930 models, in line with general pre-Depression thinking, were longer, heavier, and more expensive than the year before. They had nine inches more wheelbase length and offered six luxurious Fleetwood bodies instead of two as in 1929. Fisher-bodied LaSalles—coupes, sedans, and a convertible—cost $2500-$3000; Fleetwoods sold for up to $4000 and included a phaeton, roadster, and cabriolet. The L-head V-8 displaced 340 cid and produced 90 bhp. A respectable total of 14,986 LaSalles was built for the 1930 model year.

Unfortunately, the deepening Depression caused the division to adopt cost-cutting measures for the 1931-33 models. As a result, LaSalle adopted the 353-cid Cadillac V-8, while the latter was given LaSalle's 134-inch-wheelbase chassis. Though LaSalle's price was reduced to around $500 less than the V-8 Cadillac's, people began to consider the senior make a better buy. Cadillac V-8 production matched LaSalle's for these years and actually exceeded it in 1931.

For 1934, Cadillac tried a new approach. Abandoning any attempt to win traditional luxury-car buyers, LaSalle was given a distinct look of its own, and priced $1000 less than the V-8 Cadillac at only $1595-$1695. An Oldsmobile 240-cid L-head straight eight with special aluminum pistons was used along with "Knee-Action"

1936 LaSalle five-passenger touring sedan

1939 LaSalle convertible coupe

front suspension. Styling was marked by a narrow rounded grille and curious portholes on the sides of the hood.

The same car and price structure were continued for 1935-36, though the 1936 engine was stroked to 248 cubic inches. LaSalle's lineup in these years was conventional: a single series including coupe, convertible, and two- and four-door sedans, all on 119/120-inch wheelbases. But the formula didn't work. Sales were only 7195 units for 1934, 8651 for 1935, and 13,004 for 1936, far below those of rival "junior editions" like the Packard One-Twenty and the Lincoln Zephyr.

In 1937, LaSalle's wheelbase was lengthened to 124 inches and its Oldsmobile straight eight was scrapped for the 322-cid V-8 used on the 1936 Cadillac Series 60. The public responded, and production rose to a record 32,000 units. In 1938, due mainly to a temporary recession, output was down again to half that figure. LaSalle was floundering, yet its cars were marvelous bargains—the '37s sold for as little as $1155.

With LaSalle going nowhere except into Buick's sales territory, GM finally dropped the make after 1940. Cadillac wasn't quite ready to abandon the LaSalle market though, so the 1941 Cadillac Series 61 effectively took LaSalle's place. LaSalle's main problem was lack of a prestige name, like Packard or Lincoln. After the war, continued production of middle-priced Packards hurt that company, but Cadillac and Lincoln wisely went back to building luxury cars only.

From the collector's standpoint, Cadillacs and La-Salles of 1930-33 are among the greatest cars of the decade. The Classic Car Club rates as Classics all pre-1934 LaSalles; all Cadillacs through 1935; and the 1936-39 60 Special, Series 75, and Twelve and Sixteen models. Most of the grander open cars are very expensive today and fetch at least $50,000. Investors and collectors of more modest means would do well to consider the rakish, nicely styled 1938-39 LaSalles and the 1940 model as well, probably the best buys of this period among Cadillac Division products.

If you can afford one, however, Bill Mitchell's magnificent 60 Special of 1938-39 (and 1940-41) is the sleeper of the line. Even today, examples in decent condition can be picked up for four-figure prices. This situation can't last long, however, and you could hardly do better than to find a few of these and hide them away. The 60 Special is bound to appreciate rapidly in value as the years pass. Not only is it a beautiful, luxurious, roadable car in its own right, it is also one of the industry's watershed designs which influenced future Cadillac and General Motors styling all out of proportion to its production volume. Since model year output was 3703 units for 1938 and 5874 for 1939, there are probably a few 60 Specials as yet undiscovered.

Readers interested in Cadillacs and LaSalles should join the Cadillac-LaSalle Club, 3340 Poplar Drive, Warren, Michigan 48091.

photo credits: *Cadillac Motor Division, General Motors Corp.*

Chevrolet

**Chevrolet Motor Division, General Motors Corporation
Detroit, Michigan**

Many vintage cars are popular today in roughly the same proportion as they were when new. Chevrolets of the 1930s found favor in their time for the same reasons they appeal to collectors today: smooth-running six-cylinder engines, attractive styling, and lots of fellow owners with whom to trade stories. Though Chevy outproduced Ford in eight years of the decade, the Model A and V-8 would give Ford an early lead in popularity among collectors in the '50s. But Chevrolet's following has been growing fast and if you count Corvette enthusiasts, Chevy may now even be ahead.

Chevrolet production first passed Ford's in 1927, when Dearborn stopped building its venerable Model T and retooled its plant in preparation for the Model A. Chevrolet's strength that year—and throughout the '30s—was its "Stove Bolt Six," also called the "Cast Iron Wonder." The nicknames stem from the engine's ¼ × 20 slotted-head bolts and cast-iron pistons—not esoteric, maybe, but wonderfully effective, and as reliable as Old Faithful.

The Chevy six was developed by engineer Ormond E. Hunt, who took his cue from an earlier design by Henry M. Crane and which had evolved into the 1926 Pontiac. The Chevy powerplant used the same 3.75-inch stroke as the Pontiac, but a larger 3.31-inch bore. This gave it a displacement of 194 cubic inches, and by 1930 this unit was producing an even 50 horsepower. With certain improvements over time, this solid overhead-valve engine remained the standard Chevy powerplant for nearly three decades. For the 1933 Eagle and 1934 Master series it was given a new combustion chamber, a four-inch stroke, the name "Blue Flame Six," and was rated at 80 horsepower. Then in 1937, it was fully redesigned. Bore and stroke became nearly square at 3.50 × 3.75 inches for a displacement of 216.5 cubic inches. The 1937 powerplant also had four, instead of three, main bearings, and was shorter and lighter than its predecessor. It was behind one of these engines in 1940 that a young Juan Manuel Fangio won the car-breaking 5900-mile road race from Buenos Aires, Argentina to Lima, Peru and back with an average speed of 53.6 mph. Fangio continued to race his Chevy after World War II but eventually switched to Grand Prix cars, and became a legendary five-time world champion.

Throughout its history, Chevrolet has usually made the right decisions at precisely the right time. After he'd introduced the Stove Bolt Six, Chevy general manager William "Big Bill" Knudsen assigned the styling to Harley Earl. The result was a line of elegant-looking little cars for 1929-31 with looks that resembled a scaled-down Cadillac, but mounted on 107- to 109-inch wheelbases. In 1930 and 1931, a single series consisting of roadsters for two or four passengers, a phaeton, three coupes, and two sedans was offered at $495 to $685.

Each year's Chevys were identified by a special name: Universal in 1930, Independence in 1931, Confederate in 1932, Eagle (deluxe) and Mercury (standard) in 1933. Styling developed along the lines of the more expensive GM cars. The '33s, with their skirted fenders and graceful lines, were perhaps the most attractive Chevrolets of the entire decade. Body styles proliferated, and included such exotics as a $640 landau phaeton in 1932. The 1933 Eagles had many features designed to win buyers from Ford: a Fisher

1930 Chevrolet Universal AD two-door coach

1931 Chevrolet Independence AE three-window coupe

1932 Chevrolet Confederate BA Deluxe sports roadster

Chevrolet

body with "No-Draft Ventilation," airplane-type instruments, Cadillac-style hood doors, a cowl vent, synchromesh transmission, selective free-wheeling, safety plate glass, adjustable driver's seat, and even an octane selector. Many of these features were also carried on the standard Mercury line, which sold for no more than $475. These were good years for the division despite the prevailing Depression. Chevy production outpaced Ford's each year from 1931 to 1934. Output bottomed out at 300,000 units in 1932, rose to 480,000 in 1933, and was back to the 1931 level of 600,000 cars by 1934.

In 1934, along with new streamlined body styling, came a vital decision: "Knee-Action" independent front suspension would be offered for the Master series. This was Bill Knudsen's last act before leaving as general manager in October, 1933. According to writer Karl Ludvigsen, suspension engineer Maurice Olley tried to discourage Knudsen from using Knee-Action on the high-volume Chevy. Olley said there weren't enough centerless grinding machines in America to produce the necessary coil springs. Knudsen replied that this was just what the machine tool

industry needed to get back on its feet, but nevertheless, he restricted Knee-Action to the Master series only. Not every Master buyer liked the suspension, however. From 1935 through 1940, Masters with solid front axles were also offered at $20 less than Knee-Action models. Standards continued to use the solid axle, and Knee-Action didn't spread throughout the line until 1941.

The 1935 Chevrolets were the last models with any styling relationship to the classic era. A wide model lineup was offered. Masters sold for $560-$695, and standards were priced at $465-$550. While standards kept a 107-inch wheelbase, Masters used a 113-inch span and very rakish bodies with V-shaped windshields and streamlined fenders. The raked-back radiator had its cap concealed under the hood—an innovation at the time. Though the same Blue Flame engine was used on all models, that in the standards developed only 74 bhp. This dual-range marketing approach worked in the showrooms: Production rose to 793,000 units. Ford built more cars than Chevy in 1935, but it was the last time Dearborn would do so until 1959.

Continued modernization occurred in 1936 as Chevrolets adopted the rounded styling of the streamlined school. They had die-cast waterfall grilles, steel-spoked wheels (wires remained optional), smooth fen-

1933 Chevrolet Eagle (Master) CA sport coupe

1934 Chevrolet Master DA town sedan

1935 Chevrolet Master Deluxe two-door coach

1936 Chevrolet Master Deluxe two-door coach

1937 Chevrolet Master Deluxe two-door coach

1938 Chevrolet Master Deluxe town sedan

1939 Chevrolet Master Deluxe town sedan

ders and body lines, and all-steel "Turret Top" bodies. A big plus in the continuing battle against Ford was Chevy's new hydraulic brakes. Ford failed to adopt hydraulics until 1939, mainly due to the stubbornness of Henry Ford. The year also saw Chevy's two series become more alike as both used the 80-bhp Stove Bolt Six. The dated phaeton model was dropped. Standards, now on a 109-inch wheelbase, were offered in coupe, cabriolet, coach, sedan, town sedan, and sport sedan form. The Master series had mostly the same styles, but substituted a sport coupe for the cabriolet. The Master didn't offer a cabriolet until 1937, and even then it came with a beam front axle rather than the Knee-Action suspension.

With the new 216.5-cid 85-bhp engine for 1937, Chevrolet was particularly well equipped for the sales battle. Although production had reached 975,000 units in 1936, it slipped to 868,000 for 1937 because of a recession that year—but that tally was still 20,000 units ahead of Ford's. Model names were now altered: Master designated the lower-priced line ($619-$725), and Master Deluxe was the tag for the more costly series ($685-$788). All models rode a 112.3-inch wheelbase. Styling became rather dull as it did for several other GM cars that year. Grilles were skinny and uninteresting; bodies were high and bulky. Chevys looked pretty clumsy in the closing years of the decade, particularly compared to the increasingly streamlined Fords. Still, Chevrolet continued to outproduce Ford. In the recession year of 1938, its 490,000 units led Ford by 80,000; in 1939, the total of 648,000 cars was 116,000 more that Dearborn's.

It wasn't until 1940 that Bill Mitchell, Harley Earl, and company produced a Chevrolet with styling equal in impact to that of the elegant 1933 model. Though the 1940 Chevy shared much of its general shape with its immediate predecessors, it had just the right detail touches to make it a stand out. Again, Chevrolets looked like junior Cadillacs. Perhaps this was why Chevy again outsold Ford by 300,000 cars that year.

This styling history should be important to the collector because classic-car enthusiasts generally agree that the most colorful, dashing, genuinely beautiful Chevys of the period are those built from 1930-1933. The 1934-35 models are relatively uninteresting, except for the collectible low-production phaetons. The 1936-39 cars are even more boring, if that's possible, at least from a design viewpoint.

There is more to the story than styling, of course. Every Chevrolet during the '30s was progressively better in engineering than its predecessor. Knee-Action in 1934, Turret Tops in mid-decade, the new Six in 1937—all were important to the technical progress of the make. Nevertheless, the desirable Chevys of the 1930s are those built during the first four years. If you find them pricey today (and they are), the next place to look for collector and investment value is 1940.

Chevrolets of the '30s are welcomed by the Vintage Chevrolet Club, Post Office Box T, Atascadero, California 93422.

photo credits: *Chevrolet Motor Division, General Motors Corp.*

Chrysler

Chrysler Division, Chrysler Corporation
Detroit, Michigan

A first-hand glimpse of Walter Percy Chrysler is provided by the great coachbuilder Ray Dietrich, who headed Chrysler styling in the late 1930s: "Like Edsel Ford, Mr. Chrysler was a gentleman," Dietrich remembers. "There was dynamite in his step, his walk, his smile, and his piercing blue eyes. Like Edsel, he would never doubt what you were saying, but he was always trying to get more out of you. In later life he told me that if the damn engineers would leave him alone he'd be able to enjoy himself a lot more. Every time he'd ask for something they'd say he couldn't get it."

But that was in later life. When Walter P. built his first Chrysler in 1924, he had instrumental assistance from his three most famous engineers: Fred Zeder, Carl Breer, and Owen Skelton. This trio continued to dominate the design of Chrysler products throughout the '30s. Chrysler built some spectacular automobiles early in the decade, and its 1934 Airflow was an innovation, if not a sales success.

The 1924 high-compression Chrysler Six had laid a foundation for the company's early sales success. Its 202-cid, seven-main-bearing L-head engine developed 68 horsepower—and 0.3 bhp per cubic inch was almost revolutionary in the early '20s. The car also had four-wheel hydraulic brakes, full-pressure lubrication, attractive styling, and a price tag of around $1500. It couldn't miss. Over 32,000 Chryslers were sold in 1924. By 1927, production had reached a record 182,000 units.

Sixes continued to power all Chryslers through 1930. In that year, four different engines were built, ranging in displacement from 195.6 to 309.3 cubic inches. The smallest of these was a four-main-bearing unit with 62-65 horsepower, used on the cheap CJ model. The others were all based on the original high-compression engine and powered (in order of increasing poshness) the 66, 70, 77, and Imperial. Respective wheelbases were 109, 112, 116, 124, and 136 inches which spanned every popular size. There were no less than 28 individual models. Base sedan prices were: CJ at $845, 66 at $1095, 70 at $1445, 77 at $1495, and Imperial at $3075.

The Chrysler Imperial was conceived more as a prestige leader than a high money-earner and reached its pinnacle in 1931. It featured Chrysler's first eight—a smooth, low-revving 385 cubic-inch L-head with nine main bearings. This engine was capable of propelling the nearly 5000 pounds of this car to 96 mph, or from 0 to 60 mph in 20 seconds. But what was most distinctive—and distinguished—about the 1931 Imperials was their styling: long and low, with gracefully curved fenders and a rakish grille strongly resembling Duesenberg's. The Custom Imperial roadster priced at $3220 was some $300 less costly than a Packard Deluxe Eight, yet its 145-inch wheelbase was 21 inches longer than the Packard's. Imperials provided glorious motoring at a surprisingly low price, but the Depression kept 1931 sales down to only 3228. Coachwork was available from Locke, Derham, Murphy, Waterhouse, and LeBaron. In design, these cars were flawless—the most beautiful Chryslers ever built.

On a more plebian level for 1931, Chrysler also introduced an eight-cylinder engine on its CD series, priced about half as much as the Imperials. The CD's 240 cubic-inch engine produced 82 horsepower, and the car sat on a 124-inch-wheelbase chassis. There were several lines of Chrysler Sixes, which had 195.6, 218, and 282-cid engines. Also for 1931, Chrysler debuted "Floating Power" (rubber engine mounts) on all models, which had automatic spark control, free-wheeling transmission, and rustproofed bodies as

1930 Chrysler CI Six roadster

1932 Chrysler CI Six roadster

CONSUMER GUIDE®

1932 Chrysler Custom Imperial CL Eight convertible sedan

well. Interiors were lavish, especially on Imperials and Chrysler Eights, which featured a comprehensive set of instruments set into a polished walnut panel. Walnut was also used for the interior moldings of these cars. Welded steel bodies were another innovation in 1931, and to prove their strength, Chrysler got a five-ton elephant to stand on a sedan at Coney Island (happily, the body held). Another feature of early '30s Chryslers was an optional four-speed transmission, though it was more than the cars really needed. Basically, it was a three-speed unit with an extra-low first gear; since hardly anyone used "emergency low" this gearbox was dropped after 1933. Chrysler continued its 1931 models in 1932-33 with few changes.

Engineering has always been Chrysler's strong suit. As recently as the early 1970s, company advertising claimed that most people immediately "think engineering" when anyone mentions Chrysler. So it isn't surprising that the 1934 Chrysler Airflow was a product of engineers. What *was* curious was that canny businessman Walter Chrysler approved the Airflow concept without first considering whether the public would go for it. And that amounted to Chrysler's (the man's and the company's) first serious mistake.

As the story goes, engineer Carl Breer got the idea for a streamlined automobile when he saw a squadron of Army Air Corps planes flying overhead in 1927. Back at the factory, Breer got together with Fred Zeder and Owen Skelton to consider an automobile employing aircraft-type design principles. Wind tunnel tests suggested its shape: a basic teardrop which was altered to allow for the hood and windshield. A forward-mounted engine (it rested directly over the front axle) afforded considerable interior space and a strong beam-and-truss body provided rigidity without sacrificing room. The Airflow's seats were 50 inches wide, which was pretty impressive for 1934. It had more head, hip, shoulder, and legroom than even big Walter Chrysler

needed. Exterior styling, by Oliver Clark, followed the dictates of the engineers with a waterfall grille, flush-mounted headlights, and sharply curved fenders.

To protect itself with a traditional-style model, Chrysler produced a line of square-rigged Model CA sixes for 1934 on 118- and 121-inch wheelbases, priced around $800-$1000. All its other models were Airflows, and all of them were eight-cylinder cars. The standard Airflow Eight used a five-main-bearing 299-cid engine with 122 bhp and rode a 123-inch wheelbase; the Airflow Imperial had a new 323.5-cid engine with 130 bhp and 137.5-inch wheelbase; the Airflow Custom Imperial had the big nine-main-bearing 385-cid engine which produced 150 bhp, and rested on a huge 146.5-inch wheelbase. The Custom Imperial was the best-looking Airflow because its long wheelbase allowed the rounded body to be stretched out more. From an aesthetic point of view, it needed every inch of stretch it could get.

There was nothing wrong with the Airflow's cost. Base price of the Eight sedan was $1345, the Imperial was priced at $1625, and the Custom Imperial listed at $2245. The cars also performed well. At Bonneville in

1934 Chrysler CA Six brougham

Chrysler

1934, an Airflow Imperial coupe ran 95.7 mph for the flying-mile and 90 mph for 500 miles, capturing 72 national speed records in the process. Airflows were not flimsy, either: In Pennsylvania, one was purposely driven off a 110-foot cliff; it landed wheels down and was driven away. The Airflow's main problem was its strange new shape—and its initial scarcity in Chrysler showrooms.

Because of the considerable retooling necessary to convert to Airflow production, Chrysler delayed the cars' debut until January 1934; the Custom Imperials didn't arrive until June. Lack of cars at dealerships blunted public interest and created rumors that the Airflow was a problem child, a lemon. Sales were underwhelming. For the 12 months of 1934, Chrysler built 11,292 Airflows—against 25,252 cheap, conventional CA Sixes. In a year which saw most companies increase production by up to 60 percent from rock-bottom 1933, Chrysler's volume was up only 20 percent and the division continued to lag behind its competitors for several years. With 71,295 cars for calendar 1936, Chrysler dropped out of the top ten in the production race.

Detroit's lead times are long and it takes several years to alter a plan once it's in motion. Chrysler had banked heavily on the Airflow's success to inspire the design and sales of its cheaper makes. For 1935 and 1936, in addition to the Airflow, the division offered the more conventional Airstream series which consisted of Sixes and Eights on wheelbases of 118 and 121 inches, respectively. Though they were not pure Airflow in design, their bodies had pontoon fenders, raked-backed radiators, and teardrop headlamp pods. Overall, there was a strong family resemblance between the two lines, yet the Airstreams weren't so far out as to turn off customers completely. They carried the division in those years. Meanwhile, Chrysler built only 7751 Airflows in 1935, 6275 in 1936, and 4600 in 1937.

The bulk of Chrysler's models in 1937, and all of them in 1938, were of a transitional styling period sometimes called the "age of the potato." These included the Royal Six (with a wheelbase of 116-133 inches), the Imperial Eight (121 inches), and the Custom Imperial (140 inches). All the Eights were five-main-bearing side-valve units (the nine-main-bearing engine had disappeared after 1934). Chrysler moved back up into 10th place in production for calendar year 1937, but the recession of 1938 pushed output down to the 40,000 level for that year and again, Chrysler finished 11th. In 1939, when it built 68,000 cars, the

1934 Chrysler Airflow CU six-passenger sedan

1936 Chrysler Airstream C-7 business coupe

1935 Chrysler Airflow Imperial C-2 sedan

1937 Chrysler Royal C-16 rumble-seat coupe

1938 Chrysler Imperial C-19 five-passenger sedan

1939 Chrysler New Yorker C-23 five-passenger sedan

division dropped to 12th place in the industry. Its recovery to a 100,000 annual unit volume was only beginning when World War II closed down domestic passenger car production in early 1942.

The 1937-38 Chryslers wore barrel grilles, round fenders, and pod-type headlamps. Dashboards were ornate and varied; instruments were grouped in front of the driver for 1937, and in a central dash panel for 1938. The Royal Six, Imperial, and Custom Imperial Eights soldiered on in both years. A new model for 1938 was the New York Special, a hybrid car which used the Royal's 119-inch wheelbase and the Imperial's 229-cid-eight-cylinder engine. Distinguished by its color-keyed interior, the New York Special came only as a $1376 four-door sedan. A business coupe was planned but not produced.

The Chrysler line was fully redesigned in 1939 by Ray Dietrich. Headlamps were moved stylishly into the fenders, the barrel-shaped front end was de-emphasized by a lower grille composed of vertical bars, and all four fenders were elongated. Maintaining its reputation for sound engineering, Chrysler introduced "Superfinish," a process of mirror-finishing engine and chassis components to produce a minimum of friction.

Several now-familiar model names appeared in 1939: the Windsor (a six-cylinder sub-series of the Royal), the New Yorker, and the Saratoga. The Royal and Royal Windsor comprised series C-22, powered by the 241.5-cid, 95/102-bhp six from 1938. All models used a 119-inch wheelbase except for the seven-passenger sedan and limousine, which had a longer

wheelbase. The New Yorker and Saratoga joined the Imperial in series C-23 on a 125-inch wheelbase. The top-line C-24 chassis with a 144-inch wheelbase carried the Custom Imperial. All eight-cylinder cars had the same engine of 323.5 cubic-inch capacity, now with 135 bhp. This powerplant dated back to 1934, and would continue to be used in Chrysler Eights until the introduction of the hemi-head V-8 in 1951. Sedan prices for 1939 were: Royal $1010, Royal Windsor $1075, Imperial $1198, New Yorker $1298, Saratoga $1443, and Custom Imperial $2595.

Walter Chrysler died in August, 1940, but not before he had turned over the presidency of his company to his chosen successor, K. T. Keller, in 1935. Engineers continued to run Chrysler in the late '30s and although its cars became more conservative after the Airflow debacle, they were soundly built, reasonably well styled for the period, and offered good value.

Recognized as Classics today are all the 1930-32 Imperials, the 1933 Custom Imperial, and the 1934-35 long-wheelbase Airflow Custom Imperials. Pre-Airflow Imperials represent the collector's blue chips and LeBaron-bodied Custom Imperials are the cream of this crop.

The largest Chrysler marque group is the W.P.C. (Walter P. Chrysler) Club, Post Office Box 4705, North Hollywood, California 91607.

photo credits: *Chrysler Historical Collection*

Cord
Auburn Automobile Company, Auburn, Indiana

One can only hope to avoid criticism, a wise man once wrote, by saying nothing, doing nothing, and being nothing. Erret Lobban Cord handily avoided all those pitfalls, and he was criticized a lot. Born in 1894, the industry's golden boy (or unwelcome intruder, depending on whose opinion you hear) came literally from nowhere. A roustabout Los Angeles used-car salesman in 1920, Cord had become president and chief stockholder of Auburn by 1926. By the early '30s he owned Duesenberg and Checker, as well as Auburn, plus a host of other industrial enterprises. His method of gaining control in a business was all too clear: He dumped large quantities of common stock until its value was so low he could buy controlling interest for a song. When Cord left for England in 1934, he left to avoid an SEC investigation, not for a holiday. When he returned in 1937, it was to close the doors on three Classic marques. Few enthusiasts have forgiven him for that.

But during his wheeling-dealing decade of success, E. L. Cord was responsible for some of the most magnificent cars ever to put tire to road. Take 1929, for example. In that one year, Cord introduced three significant Classics: the Auburn cabin speedster, the Model J Duesenberg, and the front-wheel-drive Cord L-29. The L-29 proved to be rather less than its backers had hoped, but eventually it led to the Cord 810 and 812, which are among the most memorable cars of the late '30s.

The spirit of uninhibited optimism in the '20s saw many auto manufacturers expand with new models, and even new makes. Ford bought Lincoln and turned it into a rival for Cadillac and Packard. Chrysler bought Dodge, and then launched Plymouth and DeSoto. General Motors' various divisions introduced the Pontiac, Viking, Marquette, and LaSalle. Nash built the Ajax, Hudson the Essex, and Willys the Whippet. Even

in the esoteric market inhabited by E. L. Cord's cars, there seemed to be a price gap between the eight-cylinder Auburn and the mighty Duesenberg. Cord's gap-filler was a rakish new model bearing his own name and the unorthodox feature of front-wheel drive.

The L-29 was designed by racing car builder Harry Miller and Detroit engineer Cornelius Van Ranst, both avid proponents of the "horse-pulls-cart" principle. Their engine was based on Auburn's 198.6-cid straight eight, with 115 bhp at 3300 rpm, but it was not a carbon copy of the Auburn unit. For the Cord's front-drive chassis application, it had to be turned around 180 degrees so that the clutch, flywheel, and chain drive faced forward. The cylinder head was altered so that a water outlet would be up front, and the crankcase was changed to accept a rear engine mount so the powerplant would bolt up to the L-29 frame. According to Cord authority Robert Fabris, more than 70 parts of the L-29 engine were not interchangeable with those of the Auburn unit.

The L-29's three-speed sliding-pinion transmission was mounted between the clutch and differential, following the practice of a 1927 Miller Indianapolis racer. The brakes were also Miller-designed: inboard-mounted Lockheed hydraulics. Front suspension was by quarter-elliptic leaf springs, and by semi-elliptics at the rear with Houdaille-Hershey shock absorbers all around. The driveshaft to each front wheel used Cardan constant-velocity joints.

This layout was not without its disadvantages. Owing to the distance between the front wheels and the cowl, the L-29's wheelbase was a tremendous 137.5 inches. The unorthodox gearbox/differential placement and long straight-eight engine put more than half the car's weight over its rear wheels, where it did nothing for traction, and L-29s were notoriously twitchy over any kind of loose surface. The universal joints weren't up to the pounding of the front-wheel drivetrain and wore out with merciless frequency. Miller and Van Ranst could have licked these problems if they had more time, but Cord was anxious that the car debut before 1930.

However, the styling of the L-29 was sensational. All that length from front wheels to cowl allowed body engineer John Oswald to create a flowing hood and fenders that looked about 20 feet long. Auburn chief designer Al Leamy applied a Duesenberg-type radiator grille which added to the impressive appearance. For 1930, the L-29 was priced from $3095 to $3294 and was offered as a convertible cabriolet, sedan, phaeton, and brougham. The same model lineup continued in 1931-32, but prices were cut $800 across the board to spark lagging sales.

Sales didn't spark. Aside from the L-29's lack of traction and its U-joint wear problem, the front-wheel-

1930 Cord L-29 convertible cabriolet

1936 Cord 810 Beverly sedan

1936 Cord 810 Westchester sedan

1937 Cord 812 Sportsman convertible coupe

drive idea was difficult to sell to buyers in the conservative $3000 market. Furthermore, against the powerful Packards, Lincolns, and Cadillacs, the L-29 was a pig. Acceleration from 0 to 60 mph took over 30 seconds, and the car's top speed was barely 75 mph. One writer has optimistically described this performance as "pleasant tepidity," which is excusable only because it is easy to be overwhelmed by the car's styling. At the time, Cord couldn't give away the L-29. A used-car price guide published in 1935 quoted a cash value of $145 for the L-29 convertible which had sold for $3295 just five years earlier.

Historically, the L-29 is a CCCA-rated Classic. Technically, it is a sort of primitive forefather of the Olds Toronado. In its time, it was a dismal failure. When production ended early in 1932, the L-29 count barely exceeded 4400 units and the Cord name went into limbo for the next three years.

In 1936, it returned on the model 810, one of the most beautiful cars of all time. Like the L-29, the 810 had front-wheel drive but there was one key difference in the layout. The L-29 mounted its long straight-eight engine behind the transmission and both sat far behind the front axle. The 810's engine, on the other hand, was located just aft of the axle and the differential/clutch assembly extended forward to the transmission which was located ahead of the axle line. Also, the 810 used a V-8 engine which was approximately half the

length of the L-29's straight eight. The overall result was much more even weight distribution than in the L-29.

The 810's suspension consisted of independent front trailing arms with a single transverse leaf spring and constant-velocity U-joints. Its transmission was a four-speed unit with electric pre-selector. You selected the next gear by means of a lever located on an extension of the steering column; then, when you were ready, you stabbed the clutch to make the shift.

The 810's Lycoming V-8 displaced 288.6 cubic inches and was near square at 3.50×3.75 inches bore and stroke. It produced 125 bhp at 3500 rpm or, with the Schwitzer-Cummins centrifugal supercharger also

1936 Cord 810 Westchester sedan

Cord

offered in 1936, 170 bhp at 4200 rpm. Almost immediately, a higher-boost blower was fitted, which brought output up to 190. An unblown Cord would do 90 mph and 0 to 60 mph in 20 seconds. The blown version would do nearly 110 mph and 0 to 60 in 13 seconds—performance which made it one of the fastest prewar American production cars.

All this good engineering seems almost superfluous compared to the Cord's body design, developed by Gordon Buehrig, Dale Cosper, Dick Roberson, and Paul Laurenzen. Initially, the shape was proposed for a junior Duesenberg which never made it into production, but whatever its origins, the styling of the 810 was unforgettable. The smoothly formed "coffin-nosed" hood, wraparound radiator louvers, exposed exhaust pipes, and clean side elevation were faultless design elements. Its turned-metal dash with functional needle gauges was one of the most beautiful ever to grace an automobile. The 810 also bristled with innovations. Concealed headlights (electrically operated) were a first on any production car. Dual taillights with a separate license plate light, full wheel covers, a roof-mounted radio speaker, and a hidden gasoline cap also seemed quite futuristic in 1936.

The 125-inch wheelbase Cord 810 came in four models: Westchester and Beverly sedans (the main difference between them was their upholstery patterns), the Sportsman two-passenger coupe, and a four-passenger phaeton-sedan (convertible victoria). In 1937, the model designation was 812 and two long sedans on a 132-inch wheelbase were added to the line, the Custom Beverly and Custom Berline. Cord also built a handful of hardtop coupes and speedsters. With prices in the low $3000s, the cars were expensive—but worth every penny.

E. L. Cord's empire collapsed in 1937, and the Cord automobile with it. Only 1174 model 810s and 1146 model 812s were built. While the L-29 was ignored by collectors for years, the 810 and 812 began appreciating in value almost immediately after production ceased. People knew about their collectibility in the 1940's—a time when few prewar cars were regarded as more than rolling scrap metal. From the '50s on, the 810/812 was hailed as one of the all-time automotive greats. Its acceptance was due largely to the efforts of the Auburn-Cord-Duesenberg Club, founded in 1952. The club's address is Post Office Box 217, Skippack, Pennsylvania 19474.

The L-29 began to appreciate in value as a result of the classic-car boom in the '50s, and today, a pristine example will cost you $40,000 or more. A Cord 810 or 812, on the other hand, may cost little more than half that much. It only goes to show that you can ask—and get—a small fortune for anything with a Duesenberg grille and clamshell fenders, even if it can't get out of its own way.

photo credits: *Nicky Wright; Motor Vehicle Manufacturers Association*

1937 Cord 812 Sportsman convertible coupe

1937 Cord 812 phaeton-sedan

1937 Cord 812 Supercharged Beverly sedan

DeSoto

DeSoto Division, Chrysler Corporation
Detroit, Michigan

Introduced in the late 1920s to fill a market gap between Dodge and Chrysler, DeSoto was the orphan child of Walter Chrysler's corporation. Its sales were nearly always the lowest of the company's four makes: Only twice in its 33-year history did DeSoto outsell Chrysler. Its best prewar production total was less than 100,000 units and DeSoto didn't really achieve high-volume production until the 1950s.

DeSoto's technical history in the '30s parallels Chrysler's, with one exception: While Chrysler retained a conventional model in its 1934 line, DeSoto relied exclusively on the Airflow. The result was a sales disaster. By the middle of the decade, it was even money whether DeSoto would survive or wither away.

The 1930-33 models reflected general Chrysler Corporation design trends. The 1930-31s were formal, bolt-upright styles, while the 1932-33s were modified somewhat with a barrel-like grille. Both six and eight-cylinder engines were offered from 1930 through 1932, and all were conventional side-valve units. The five-main-bearing DeSoto eight displaced 207.7 cubic inches and produced 70 bhp. In mid-1931, it was stroked to 220.7 cid, which provided 77 bhp, and it remained in this form for the balance of 1931 and 1932. All DeSoto Eights used a 114-inch wheelbase. The model lineup comprised a roadster, phaeton, convertible, two coupes, and two sedans; in 1932, a touring model replaced the phaeton. The DeSoto eight was a smoother, quieter engine than the DeSoto six, but neither was a powerhouse. Eights appealed to about one in three DeSoto customers. After the eights disappeared, DeSoto did not build another one until the hemi-head "Firedome" V-8 of 1952.

DeSoto's meat and potatoes were its sixes: cast-iron, side-valve, four-main-bearing engines based on (but smaller than) their Chrysler counterparts. The

1930 version was a 175-cid unit with 57 bhp, which grew to 190 cid and 60 bhp in April, 1930. Gradually, it was further increased in size and power: 205.3 cid and 67 bhp by mid-1931; 211.5 cid and 75 bhp by 1932; 217.8 cid and 82 bhp by 1933. While DeSoto Eight prices averaged around $1000 during this period, Sixes cost around $800-$850. In 1933, with sales at an all-time low, DeSoto cut prices: $665 bought a standard sedan or coupe and $875 purchased the top-line Custom convertible sedan.

In the early '30s, DeSotos were not revised for each model year. Actually, the first car to be designed that way was the "All New Six" or SC model, introduced in January, 1932. These chunky but attractive cars were priced at $775-$975. Offered were a standard sedan; a seven-passenger sedan; and a Custom sedan, convertible, and phaeton. Its 1933 successor included more coupes and a new brougham (two-door sedan) as well as the above models.

All the pros and cons of the 1934 Chrysler Airflow were also true of the DeSoto version. The latter used the largest and most powerful DeSoto six to date: 241.5 cubic inches and 100 horsepower. The engine, at least, was a survivor and remained in production (with 93 bhp in standard form, 100 bhp optional) for 1935-36. In 1937, it was destroked to 228.1 cubic inches but produced the same amount of power. Enlarged again in 1941 and 1951, it was the standard DeSoto six until the last of its kind was offered in 1954. Vice-free and reliable, it would run forever in exchange for an occasional quart of oil. Gas mileage was good—up to 22 mpg.

The 1934 DeSoto Airflow came in one series on a 115.5-inch wheelbase. Just four body styles were offered, each priced at $995: coupe, brougham, sedan, and town sedan. In 1935, DeSoto hastily regrouped. The Airflows were joined by the much more conventional looking (and saleable) DeSoto Airstream. The division reached downward by pricing the Airstream at $695-$825, which covered seven models, all on a 116-inch wheelbase. Airstream styling consisted of a Plymouth-like raked grille, slab sides, and a rounded deck. Sedans were offered with and without outside spare tire—"without" meant that a faired-in trunk housed the spare. There was even a $35 two-tone paint option. DeSoto sales increased 116 percent in 1935, but in the production race the division dropped to 13th place because of Packard's highly successful One-Twenty series.

The division rode out the rest of the decade with increasingly larger and duller models. The Airflows disappeared after 1936. The 118-inch standard wheelbase in 1936 was increased to 119 inches for 1938-39. Long sedans and limousines began coming off the lines in 1936, too, and by 1938, these had acquired a

1931 DeSoto Six Model SA roadster

DeSoto

136-inch wheelbase. Styling, by Dietrich, was very conservative, though it did match contemporary tastes. DeSoto finished 11th in production for calendar 1937 with a prewar record of 86,541 cars—the best it would do through 1948. The recession of 1938 cut output back to 32,688 and DeSoto finished 12th in volume. The recovery year of 1939 saw 53,269 cars, but rivals were doing much better so the division finished in 14th place.

By 1938, DeSotos had evolved into a consistent, recognizable form: Deluxes and Customs, priced at around $900 and $1000, respectively, both powered by the same engines and sharing the same conventional chassis. Long sedans and limousines were produced in each series. There weren't even any open cars in 1939, though a sliding sunroof was offered. Styling was heavily influenced by Chrysler's junior makes: A 1939 DeSoto looked like a Plymouth that had taken pep pills. Dumpy styling remained a sales problem until well after World War II.

Among collectors, DeSotos aren't exactly hot, and none are rated as Classics. However, for those seeking old-car enjoyment more than an inflation shelter, some good buys are available. Worth considering are the vintage-style open models with real radiators, circa 1930-31; about $6000 should net you a very nice roadster or phaeton. The highest amount ever paid for a DeSoto is $12,000, which only proves the old adage that a fool and his money are soon parted. The appropriate organization is the DeSoto Club of America, 105 East 96th, Kansas City, Missouri 64114.

photo credit: *Chrysler Historical Collection*

1934 DeSoto SE Airflow coupe

1936 DeSoto S1 Airstream Custom four-door sedan

1937 DeSoto S3 convertible coupe

CONSUMER GUIDE®

Doble

Doble Steam Motors Corporation, Emeryville, California

The Doble steam car is not entirely qualified for this book because it was primarily a car of the 1920s. Production was small even then, and only a handful of Dobles—the Model Fs—were built in 1930-31. Still, there is reason to overlook this fine point and take a look at the Doble. The current need for an alternative to the internal-combustion engine, which burns rapidly dwindling supplies of fossil fuel, suggests that an advanced steam car might be a welcome development. The Doble was the most advanced steam car ever conceived, and in view of today's growing energy problem, it may provide inspiration for a modern equivalent.

Abner Doble was a San Francisco technician of fastidious character—a perfectionist to the core. Fascinated with steam cars at an early age, he built his first one as a high school student using old Locomobile parts. Doble knew the famous Stanley brothers, but he was not impressed with their car. To him it was appallingly crude: It needed a better condenser and the capability of being started easily from cold. The first car Doble built from the ground up used a water-tube boiler to raise steam quickly and a special radiator which condensed all steam exhaust. The engine started fast, yet showed no escaping steam while operating. Doble demonstrated this car to the Stanleys, and within three years their cars had an efficient steam condenser, too.

Abner Doble formed and reformed several eastern companies between 1910 and 1920, none of which were successful. Moving to California in 1920, he sank his resources into a new factory and protracted research. Ultimately, this culminated in the 1924 Series E.

Doble made use of a burner connected to an electric blower which blended air with gasoline or a gas-kerosene mixture. Ignition was by battery, coil, and spark. Since steamers require intermittent ignition, Doble designed an automatic device which switched the ignition on and off, and thus controlled the operation of the burner according to the needs of the driver. To start the car, the driver first flicked on the ignition to activate the blower. The blower sucked in air and mixed it with the fuel; the mixture was then ignited by a single spark plug. At the end of this cycle, the ignition automatically switched off, while the blower continued revolving. Fuel burning continued until the steam boiler reached maximum pressure, at which point the burner switched off automatically. What all this amounted to was a combination of steam and internal combustion principles—the best of both worlds.

The Model E Doble four-cylinder engine had a 213 cubic-inch displacement and developed 125 horsepower at a mere 1300 rpm. The car's cruising speed was 75 mph and a top speed was close to 100. Against the competition of the mid '20s and early '30s, its performance was staggering. The Type H6B Hispano-Suiza, then one of the fastest production cars in the world, had a cruising speed 10-15 mph below the Doble's.

Together with its technological sophistication, the Doble offered luxury. Bodies, most often supplied by Murphy, spanned a wide variety of styles. The price of these cars was equal to their esoteric character—up to $12,000.

The last Doble was the Model F, launched in 1929 and sold through 1931 amidst corporate misfortune. The F was little changed from the Model E. The main alteration was a higher-pressure firebox surrounded with cooling water. Really, by 1930, the Doble had long been perfected. The problem was not the product, but the company.

In the mid '20s, stock manipulators were a common breed of crook, and unfortunately, Doble was one of their victims. One company went broke just after its stock was traded for Doble stock. When the first company's stock was found to be worthless, the manipulators had already sold the acquired Doble stock at a 1000-percent profit. Doble, of course, received no money from the sale. Its own stock issues were held up by the authorities, and Doble finally had to settle the claims of those who had been defrauded. The firm was already on the brink of bankruptcy in 1926; the Great Crash of 1929 merely provided the final push into the financial abyss.

Abner Doble persisted with steam engine designs for airplanes, boats, and light industrial engines. His last automobile involvement was with Robert Paxton McCulloch on the stillborn Paxton steam car of 1954, which was not produced due to lack of adequate capital. Doble died in 1961 but his principles live on, and may yet become the basis on which we build a steam car of the future. The Doble cars which survive today are certainly collector's items, and all are rated as Classics. The last time a Series E was sold, in 1976, it brought $18,000—a fairly small sum for technological perfection.

---

photo credit: *Motor Vehicle Manufacturers Association*

1930 Doble Model F roadster

Dodge

Dodge Division, Chrysler Corporation, Detroit, Michigan

Walter Percy Chrysler bought the Dodge Brothers Car Company on July 31, 1928—and he moved in fast. According to writer Beverly Kimes, Chrysler's lieutenent, K. T. Keller, was at the Dodge factory plastering up signs reading "Chrysler Corporation: Dodge Division" while the papers were being signed in New York. The next day, Dodge representative Clarence Dillon called Chrysler to advise him that the factory could run itself for the next several months. Walter P. amazed him with the reply, "Hell, Clarence, our boys moved in yesterday."

This incident represents the spirit of Chrysler's takeover of a company several times its size and, the beginning of Chrysler Corporation as it is known today. For Dodge, the rescue had come not a moment too soon. John and Horace Dodge, one-time engine suppliers to Henry Ford, built their first cars in 1914. They often ran second or third behind Ford and Willys

through the early '20s, but by 1927, Dodge sales had fallen drastically. Walter Chrysler's minions took over with a vengeance. Immediately they dropped the Dodge Four; in 1930, they added an eight-cylinder model and gave the cars some badly needed new styling.

Dodge's market position shifted around in the early '30s—prices were sometimes above and sometimes below the DeSoto's. By 1933, the Chrysler hierarchy had decreed that Dodge should occupy the attractive territory just above Plymouth and below DeSoto. Because of the Depression, it took Chrysler eight years to rebuild Dodge Division, but by 1935, Dodge was building over 200,000 cars a year. In 1937, the division set a prewar production record with 288,841 units. By then, Dodge was firmly established as the number-four producer after Chevy, Ford, and Plymouth.

The cars retained their Dodge Brothers styling

1930 Dodge DD6 four-door sedan

1932 Dodge DK rumble-seat coupe

1936 Dodge D2 "Beauty Winner" two-door touring sedan

1937 Dodge D5 seven-passenger touring sedan

1936 Dodge LC half-ton pickup truck

1938 Dodge D8 four-door touring sedan

barely long enough for Chrysler designers to alter it. Chrysler also altered the engines and experimented with a wide range of L-head sixes and eights. Dodge eights were built through 1933 in three displacements, all with a 4.25-inch stroke. Displacement of the first eight was 220.7 cubic inches with a 2.88-inch bore (1930-32). Next came a 240.3 cubic-inch unit with a 3.0-inch bore (1931-32); then 282.1 cubic inches with a 3.25-inch bore (1932-33). Horsepower figures for the three engines were 75, 84, and 90/92, respectively. Each offered a slight performance advantage over the Dodge six, but smoothness and low-end torque were their big attractions. The Eights were also more graceful than the lower-priced Sixes because they rode longer wheelbases up to 122 inches. They were not really performance cars, but were designed instead to compete with the likes of Pontiac, and offered several sporty body styles. Roadsters and phaetons, plus a convertible sedan were available in 1932-33 as well as sedans and coupes. Prices began at about $900. The highest price for any Dodge Eight in the '30s was the $1395 convertible sedan of 1933.

Dodge styling was the most conservative of any Chrysler Corporation product, and fortunately for the division, Dodge never had its version of the Airflow. Lines were four-square and upright through 1934—the only concession to the streamlining craze was a rakish grille on the 1933-34 models. The famous Dodge ram

hood ornament, a manifestation of the Chrysler take-over, first appeared in 1932. A waterfall grille and rounder, skirted fenders crept into the appearance formula for 1935 as part of Chrysler's company-wide "Airstream" look. Under the direction of body designer Ray Dietrich, Dodges adopted extended pontoon-style fenders, elongated rear decks, and a sharp-edged frontal motif in 1939. Meanwhile, the upper-priced Chrysler makes had backed away from the radical Airflow look, so that by the end of the decade Dodge had a strong family resemblance to DeSoto and Chrysler

The Dodge six—the engine foundation on which Walter Chrysler built—saw many forms in the early '30s. It ranged in displacement from 190 to 242 cubic inches, and in horsepower from 60 to 78. In 1932, an L-head six with 217.8 cubic inches was produced (although it was debored to 201.3 inches for 1933 only) and remained as the standard Dodge engine from 1934 on. Horsepower was 75 in 1932-33, and 87 bhp after 1934. Numerous six-cylinder body styles were offered encompassing all the popular open types of the period. Dodge continued the convertible sedan model throughout most of the decade. It was absent only in 1935 and was finally dropped in 1939 due to low demand. Dodge Sixes had wheelbases of 109 to 117 inches through 1939. A long-wheelbase chassis appeared in 1936 for the seven-passenger sedans and

1939 Dodge D11 "Luxury Liner" four-door sedan

Dodge

limousines, and reached 134 inches in 1939.

Chrysler would give any name to a car if it would lead to more sales. Dodge model names included such prosaic entries as the "New Standard" in 1934, the "New Value" in 1935, the "Beauty Winner" in 1936, and the "Luxury Liner" in 1939 (the last later became something of a slang expression). Sales were brisk as the Depression eased—far better than those of the Airflow-plagued Chrysler and DeSoto divisions. Dodge made a strong effort for the special-body business and sold chassis to hearse, ambulance, and sta-

1939 Dodge TC pickup truck

tion wagon builders. Dodge trucks also sold well and were decorated with pictures of everything from elephants to giant soup cans to help publicize Dodge or its customers.

One of Dodge's more innovative years was 1937. Though the cars were not vastly altered from the "Air Styled" 1936 models, they introduced non-snag door handles, recessed dash knobs, flush-mounted dash gauges, ultra-low driveshaft tunnels, one-piece steel roof construction, and built-in defroster vents. On the Series D5 for 1937, Dodge introduced the first fully insulated rubber body mountings.

The 1939s—which arrived simultaneously with the futuristic 1939 World's Fair and Dodge's Silver Anniversary—were totally redesigned. In apparent celebration of the twin events, Dodge reinstated a dual model lineup for the first time since 1934. The two series were dubbed Special and Deluxe, the main difference being in interior trim. The economic doldrums were over at last.

The same "collectibility" factors that govern DeSotos also apply to Dodges, though Dodge is probably the least sought-after Chrysler marque of the period. The Walter P. Chrysler Club, Box 4705, North Hollywood, California 91607 accepts all Dodges of the '30s. A new club devoted only to this make is Club Dodge, Box 1215, Scranton, Pennsylvania 18501.

photo credit: *Chrysler Historical Collection*

Duesenberg

Duesenberg Motor Company,
Indianapolis, Indiana

Of the Model J Duesenberg, the late Ken Purdy, famed motoring writer, once said: "It is, I think, the finest motorcar yet built in the United States. . . . I mean that its margin of superiority over its contemporaries was greater than any other domestic automobile has known." Don Vorderman, former editor of *Automobile Quarterly*, has stated: " . . the Model J is the most superlative automobile ever built. There was simply nothing on wheels that could equal its combination of technical sophistication, power output, performance, smoothness, and impeccable road manners, all dressed in a bewildering array of coachwork which ranged from blisteringly fast two-seaters to sedans, touring, and town cars of awesome opulence and elegance."

It is fairly easy to find quotes like that about many cars. It is next to impossible to find Purdy and Vorderman, two of the keenest automotive critics, agreeing so exactly. But the Duesenberg is larger than life, and those who have studied it inevitably reach for superlatives.

He that is first, as Cadillac said, must always live in the white light of publicity. The Duesenberg J has had plenty of that. It has always been the car collector's ultimate fantasy, yet it has also been called a failure by Europeans who knew nothing of its history. Long articles have been written to prove just how much horsepower it had. Mass media feature writers have composed far-out tales of Duesenbergs that cost $50,000 new—a figure which stretched the truth by a good 100 percent. And so it goes.

It is hard to discuss this subject without emotion. When the Model J was new, it was the most envied car in the world. In the 1940s and '50s, it was one of the few prewar cars to be widely coveted. By the 1960s, Duesenbergs were selling for more than they had cost new, and in the '70s, one particular car broke the record for the highest price ever paid for an automobile—several times over.

Frederick Samuel Duesenberg was born in Lippe, Germany in 1876. He emigrated to America as a child, and adopted Iowa as his home state. In his 20s, Fred built bicycles—racing bikes famed for their precision. In Des Moines in 1906, with his brother August, he designed the Mason, a car named for the brothers' backer. The Mason was succeeded by the Maytag, which expired after 1911, though that company is still famous today for its washing machines. By 1912, the Duesenbergs were starting to put together impressive racing engines. In 1917, they moved to Elizabeth, New Jersey, where they set up a factory to build these powerplants as well as engines for aircraft, tractors, boats, and other vehicles.

Duesenberg racing engines grew in prestige after World War I. A special 16-cylinder unit powered a Land

Speed Record car to 158 mph at Daytona in 1919. The only time an American car won the French Grand Prix was in 1921, and the winner was a Duesenberg racer. In the '20s, Duesenbergs won the Indianapolis 500 three times.

With their considerable experience in building complete racing cars, the Duesenberg brothers moved their factory to Indianapolis. The Model A Duesenberg appeared in late 1921 as their first production car and sold for $6500. Genuinely derived from competition experience, the Model A had a potent 259.6-cid overhead-valve straight-eight engine, and was good for 85 mph. A first among American cars was its four-wheel hydraulic brake system, something Fred Duesenberg had developed for his race cars as early as 1914. The Model A was a brilliant design and fastidiously built, but the brothers were never good businessmen. Less than 500 cars were sold through 1926, when the company was purchased by Erret Lobban Cord. In 1927, a dozen derivatives of the Model A, called the Model X,

Duesenberg SSJ speedster

Duesenberg SSJ speedster

Duesenberg

were produced, but this was just a stopgap measure. E. L. Cord wanted something far more esoteric.

The result was the Model J, introduced to universal applause in December, 1928, and the product of Fred Duesenberg's brains and E. L. Cord's money. To an appreciative public, Cord proclaimed the birth of "the world's finest motor car." By almost any measurement, it was.

In any discussion of Duesenbergs, the subject of engines and horsepower inevitably comes up. The Model J was advertised with 265 horsepower at 4250 rpm from its 420-cid Lycoming-built straight eight. This was a mind-boggling figure—easily more than twice the output of the industry's previous horsepower leader, Chrysler. Doubters have since argued that the J's actual bhp rating was closer to 200, but there is evidence the factory wasn't exaggerating. The stock Lycoming eight had a compression ratio of only 5.2:1— yet one modified engine with an 8:1 compression ratio allegedly delivered 390 bhp. Former *Road & Track* publisher John R. Bond has a famous Lycoming chart showing a *reject* Model J engine delivering 208 bhp at 3500 rpm, and he projected 245-250 bhp at the 4250 rpm rev limit. So, the odds are that the production Model J developed at least 250 horsepower.

But forget horsepower. Consider some of the mighty J's other details. Its cylinder head contained 32 valves—16 to a side or four to a cylinder. These were actuated by twin overhead camshafts driven by chains the size of ankle bracelets. The engine itself was enameled in bright green and its fittings were finished in nickel, chrome, or stainless steel. The standard 142.5-inch-wheelbase chassis used 8.5-inch deep, quarter-inch thick frame rails and oversize hydraulic brakes (vacuum assisted after 1930). Aluminum alloy was used extensively in the engine, dash, steering column, differential/pinion/flywheel housings, crankcase, camshaft, timing chain covers, water pump, intake manifold, brake shoes, and gas tank. Despite their size, most Duesies didn't weigh much over 5200 pounds so they could do a staggering 89 mph in second gear and 112-116 mph in high.

The Model J cockpit was opulent but thoroughly functional. The most comprehensive instrument panel yet seen in an automobile included a brake pressure gauge, ammeter, oil pressure gauge, tachometer, split-second stopwatch, 150-mph speedometer, gas gauge, altimeter/barometer, and water temperature gauge. Warning lights reminded the driver to add chassis oil (the chassis lubricated itself every 75 miles), to change engine oil, or to replenish battery water. The dash was typical of Fred Duesenberg's

Duesenberg J dual-cowl phaeton

Duesenberg SJ convertible coupe by LaGrande

Duesenberg SJ convertible sedan by Rollston

dedication to excellence—his insistence that the car be superior in all respects.

There's been a lot of confusion about Duesenberg prices. The bare chassis listed for $8500 in 1929-30, and $9500 in 1931. Though bodies were announced with a price as low as $2500, the lowest-price Murphy coupe actually seems to have cost $3500 minimum. The majority of Model Js sold for less than $17,000. A few sold for up to $20,000, and a tiny handful for up to $25,000. Even so, given equivalent dollar values, most of these prices would be well above the most expensive production cars available today, and roughly 20 times the price of the contemporary Model A Ford.

Duesenberg bodies were as regal as their drivetrains. They were, after all, designed not as sports cars but as *grand luxe* carriages, so they used the finest woods, fabrics, and leathers money could buy. Vanity cases, radios, bars, and rear instrument panels were all commonplace features. One town car was upholstered in silk, trimmed in ebony, and had ivory and silver fittings. Another car reportedly had solid gold hardware and inlaid mosaic wood in the rear compartment; its owner covered the floor with an oriental prayer rug worth more than the car itself. Despite its astonishing performance, the J remained primarily an ultra-luxurious automobile capable of running at any speed in eerie silence, as its customers demanded.

Who were those demanding customers? Since only 470 J chassis and 480 engines were built between 1929 and 1936, it's safe to say they went to a fairly exclusive clientele. Duesie advertising pinpointed those buyers. Typically, the ad contained not one word of hype or any specifications—not even a picture of the car. Instead, it might illustrate a yachtsman, commanding his boat against what looked like a 40-knot gale; or a smoking-jacketed tycoon relaxing in a library that would do justice to a university. In all the ads, a single line of type would read, "He Drives a Duesenberg." The factory was not at all chauvanistic, however. One ad showed an elegantly attired lady, conferring with a hat-in-hand gardener; in the background are gardens that would put Versailles to shame. "She Drives a Duesenberg," read the predictable title.

Between 1932 and 1935, Duesenberg ran off 36 supercharged models, the Series SJ, with the chassis priced at $11,750. The centrifugal supercharger delivered five psi of boost at 4000 rpm, and the engine used tubular-steel connecting rods instead of the aluminum-alloy variety. The first SJs developed 320 horsepower but August Duesenberg, in a search for more power, half-heartedly tried a set of manifolds with a "rams horn" configuration. He was amazed to see output jump to 400 bhp—and so was everyone else.

The performance of the Duesenberg SJ is well documented. A stock model would do 104 mph in second gear and had a top speed of 140 mph. Using a light

Duesenberg SJN "Twenty Grand" sedan by Rollston

Duesenberg SJN convertible coupe by Rollston

Duesenberg JN convertible sedan by Rollston

Duesenberg

roadster body, but no mechanical modifications, an SJ piloted by Ab Jenkins went to Bonneville in late 1934. For 24 hours Jenkins averaged 135 mph; for one hour he averaged 152, and toward the end he did one lap at 160 mph. The SJ was simply astonishing.

The point must be made again that all this performance was looked upon with relative disdain by the company. "If a 70-mph car is driven 65 mph, the whole mechanism is working so hard, like a runner out of breath, that critical motorists, at least, must object to its effort," read the Model J brochure. ". . . the maximum speed of the Duesenberg is so high that even 100 mph cannot be regarded as particularly hard work . . . rates of 40 and 60 mph are loafing speeds."

Yet there's more to the Duesenberg story than power and luxury. Despite its size, the car had balance, precision, finesse. The heaviness so often displayed by the Duesie's high-priced domestic and imported contemporaries was absent. It was not "trucky;" it did not steer like a tank; the clutch pedal did not take a Purdue football player to depress; the vacuum-servo brakes were more than adequate. The car did understeer, but its exquisitely accurate steering allowed this to be corrected easily. With its exhaust cut-out open, an SJ throbbed with a din even extroverts couldn't long endure; but with the cut-out closed, it was little louder than a healthy Cadillac Sixteen.

The only Duesenbergs that could genuinely be called sports cars were two specials, unofficially titled SSJ. They were built by E. L. Cord's Union City Body Company, usually known as La Grande, and had 125-inch wheelbases. The first was bought right off the showroom floor by Gary Cooper; the second was purchased by Clark Gable, who evidently couldn't bear the thought of being outclassed by his friend. There is no definite information on how these cars performed, and though both survive today, their current owners are understandably reluctant about giving demonstration

Duesenberg 1932 Indianapolis 500 race car

drives. But with a chassis 17 inches shorter than standard and relatively lean bodies, the SSJ's flat-out behavior must have been devastating. They were also among the most beautiful Duesenbergs ever built.

Another low-production offshoot was the JN in 1935, of which ten were built, all with Rollston coachwork. A converse to the SSJ, the JN used a longer wheelbase of 153.5 inches. It had smaller wheels (17 instead of 19 inches) and skirted fenders. But its main characteristic was a very low body drawn down below the frame rails. Of the ten JNs built, two received the supercharged engine and the logical designation SJN. But again, there is a lot of confusion. Some SJs have been relieved of their superchargers, while a few blowers have been added to unsupercharged Js. (A longtime legend among the uninformed was that any car with outside exhaust pipes had a supercharger, like the classic Auburns, Cords, and Mercedes. Like Auburn, far more Duesies with that beautiful external plumbing were unblown than blown.)

As a company, Duesenberg was never meant to make money, only "the world's finest motor car," so it wasn't seriously damaged by the business slowdown of the Depression. It continued to plod along, building its magnificent cars on a cost-no-object basis, the prestige line among E. L. Cord's automobiles. The factory finally folded when Cord's business empire collapsed in 1937. The last Duesenberg was ordered by German artist Rudolf Bauer early that year. Its chassis was assembled by the Chicago dealership after the Indianapolis factory closed its doors. Because of the approaching war, the last chassis was never shipped to its owner, but Bauer eventually made his way to America and had a four-door convertible sedan body completed for it in 1940. The last Duesenberg's overall cost was $21,000.

Fred S. Duesenberg did not survive his company. He died in 1932 following an auto accident—in an SJ, sadly. His brother Augie carried on, but failed in an attempt to revive the marque in 1947. There was also an unsuccessful try in 1966. Yet another Duesenberg revival, the product of Kenneth and Harlan Duesenberg (nephews of the famed brothers) is now well underway and scheduled for very limited production in 1980.

Fred was the heart and soul of Duesenberg, and he was widely mourned. "But he died content," Ken Purdy wrote, "for 1932 was the first of the years of the locust in our day, the first year of an era that would have small place for a man who would make no slightest compromise with quality. And Fred Duesenberg had done what is given few men to do; he had chosen a good course and held unswervingly to it. . . . With his mind and his two good hands he had created something new and good and in its way immortal. And the creator is, when all is said and done, the most fortunate of men."

photo credits: *Henry Ford Museum; Ray Wolff*

Ford

Ford Motor Company, Dearborn, Michigan

ord entered 1930 with its still-popular Model A, but the car was given more major changes than in previous years. Though its basic styling remained the same, the car's most obvious alteration was its brightwork: Stainless steel replaced nickel plate on the radiator shell, and headlight shells and rims. Minor styling changes included lower and wider fenders and a higher hoodline. Ford also switched to "balloon" tires and decreased wheel size from 21 to 19 inches. Running changes in 1930 included a lower steering ratio to reduce effort at the wheel, and standardization of vacuum-operated windshield wipers. The Model A engine continued with a 200.5 cubic-inch displacement and 40 bhp.

In June, 1930, a completely new Deluxe two-door phaeton was added to the line. It was sportier than the four-door phaeton and had side-mounted spare tire, chrome-trimmed trunk rack, all-leather upholstery, and

lower steering wheel and windshield frame. Another new style, added in the autumn of 1930, was a victoria coupe. This car had no exterior sun visor but used a slanted windshield, a feature which prefigured many Model As of the following years.

There was little change to the car for 1931. A painted section appeared on the top front of the radiator shell, which makes identification easy. The cheapest Model A that year was the standard roadster priced at $435; the four-door phaeton was $5 more. Model A body types were extensive. There were three roadsters, three coupes, a cabriolet, a victoria, and six sedans—not to mention special body styles like the taxicab and town car. All these models used a 103.5-inch wheelbase.

Ford had pulled ahead of Chevrolet in 1929 and 1930, now that Model A production was in full swing. Its output of 1,155,162 cars in calendar year 1930 was its

1930 Ford Model A Victoria coupe

1930 Ford Model A two-door phaeton

1930 Ford Model A station wagon

Ford

best for the entire decade. But Ford fell behind Chevy again in 1932, caused in part by the changeover to a new engine for the majority of '32 models—the first low-priced V-8 offered in the United States.

Henry Ford had wanted to replace the faithful old Model T with a V-8 car in the 1920s, but there wasn't enough time. So, the Model A was introduced without the V-8 as an interim measure. Production of the "A" ended in the autumn of 1931, but the car was sold through April, 1932. Then, a new four-cylinder Model B was introduced. The new V-8 and Model B shared a 106.5-inch wheelbase and the same body styles—the big difference, of course, was under the hood. The V-8 was a tremendous bargain: A roadster, coupe or phaeton could be bought for less than $500. Still, some buyers preferred the four-cylinder model, which would be continued through 1934.

The cast-iron flathead V-8 engine developed 65 bhp

at 3400 rpm and displaced 221 cubic inches. The car's top speed was a relatively sensational 78 mph and caused a terrific storm of public interest. Even before it was introduced, over 50,000 orders had been received for the V-8, and millions flocked to the showrooms to see the new car in March, 1932.

Henry Ford kept a close watch over design and development of the V-8—he was always telling the engineers what to do. The need to get the car on the market quickly left insufficient time for durability testing, and some engines began to show signs of failure once the cars went into daily use. The early engines used a lot of oil; the cylinder heads developed cracks; engine mounts became loose; ignition problems occurred. Ford supplied replacement pistons by the thousands to ease the crisis, but the engine difficulties hurt sales: In both 1933 and 1934, Chevrolet continued to lead Ford by a comfortable margin.

There was a completely new look for 1933. The hood now extended back to the windshield; doors were hinged at the rear on closed body styles; fenders were skirted and dipped low in front. The wheelbase grew to

1932 Ford Model B station wagon

1932 Ford V-8 Deluxe roadster

1933 Ford V-8 Deluxe "Tudor" sedan

1934 Ford V-8 Deluxe roadster (Timmis replica)

1936 Ford Deluxe convertible touring sedan

1937 Ford Deluxe "Tudor" sedan

1939 Ford Deluxe convertible coupe

112 inches and tire size shrank to 17 inches. The speedy Ford V-8 was a favorite of many, not the least of whom was the notorious John Dillinger. Dillinger once wrote Henry Ford to tell him just how much he liked the product—an unbiased plug from Public Enemy Number-One.

Ford's V-8 engine was improved and the car's frame completely redesigned for 1933. Edsel Ford had always played an important part in styling, and the '33 design was universally applauded. At 335,000 units, Ford production was up by 100,000 cars in 1933 which, if not better than Chevrolet, was at least a decent gain.

The 1934 Ford had minor styling changes, though the 112-inch wheelbase was now locked up for the remainder of the decade. The '34 engine had a new carburetor and manifold which increased output to 85 bhp. Most of the engine problems of previous years had been eliminated by this time. One could still buy a standard two-passenger coupe for little more than $500. The Deluxe four-door ("Fordor" in company parlance) cost $615 and featured safety glass all around as standard equipment.

Also as a regular model, Ford offered a wood-bodied station wagon constructed of birch or maple. Through 1935, these were made by the Mingel Company of Kentucky and assembled by Murray or Briggs in Detroit. In 1935, Ford started to manufacture its own wagons in a plant at Iron Mountain, Michigan. It was an ideal location because hardwood forests were nearby which minimized transportation costs.

Ford styling took on a more rounded look in 1935. For the first time, an integral trunk could be had in the sedan. Horsepower remained at 85 bhp this year, as it would for the rest of the decade. Engine improvements included a new camshaft and a better crankcase ventilation system. The frame and rear axle were also beefed up. The suspension still consisted of a single transverse spring front and rear—an archaic arrangement which would remain part of Ford chassis design for another 13 years. The transverse springs and use of mechanical brakes were two areas in which Ford was distinctly behind the times, but old Henry refused to believe any of his ideas were outdated. He did abandon traditional wire wheels in favor of all-steel wheels after 1935, however.

The 1936 Ford featured minor styling changes. The hood became longer and more pointed, and the grille was given a sharper V-shape. One new body style was added, a five-passenger cabriolet, and all other styles were carried over for a combined total of 19, counting standard and Deluxe versions. The more stylish models, like convertible coupes, convertible sedans, and roadsters, came only in Deluxe form. The Deluxe four-door convertible sedan topped the price list at $780. Industry design practices dictated hiding some components that were previously visible, so the 1936

Ford

Ford's horns were placed behind catwalk grilles which followed the pattern of the radiator grille. Though the spare tire could be mounted either inside or outside on sedan models, external spares were still the rule rather than the exception.

An additional V-8 was added to the line for 1937. This was a smaller engine than the 85-bhp V-8 displacing just 136 cubic inches and yielding 60 horsepower. The engine had originally been conceived for use in European-market Fords because the European tax structure was based on displacement (in Britain, on bore but not stroke). The V-8/60, therefore, had a much reduced bore compared to the V-8/85 (2.6 versus 3.1 inches). Also for 1937, the larger V-8 had a relocated water pump, which made a vast improvement to the cooling system. It also had larger insert bearings and new cast alloy steel pistons.

Car prices had been on the rise, so the smaller V-8 gave Ford added market coverage. Bodies were now of all-steel construction: Closed cars had a steel roof instead of the cloth insert as in years past. Evidence of Ford's attempts at streamlining was ample. The headlamps were now incorporated into the front fenders; the grille was stretched and sloped backwards at the top; fine horizontal grillework decorated the front end and hood sides. The 1937 Ford was one of the handsomest cars of the decade—even President Franklin Roosevelt bought a convertible sedan to use at his Warm Springs, Georgia retreat. In a year of questionable styling for the industry as a whole, the Ford was a standout—proof that the streamlining era did not mean an end to distinctive and timelessly styled automobiles.

In fact, in the late '30s, styling was one of Ford's few strong points. By this time, Henry Ford, who brought the automobile to the masses in his youth, was a hardened man in his mid 70s. Though his son Edsel was now president of the company, Henry continued to rule Ford with an iron fist. Aside from stifling new product developments, Henry adamantly refused to let his factories unionize. His right-hand man, Harry Bennett, employed a sort of private army to ensure that Henry got his way. In 1937, men distributing union handbills took a brutal beating from Bennett's troops, resulting in the worst public image Henry Ford ever had.

Henry's strong reliance on Bennett's advice over that of his own son bothered the sensitive Edsel Ford. The strain of infighting took its toll: In 1943, Edsel would die of fever, stomach ulcers, and cancer. Ultimately, Henry's wife threatened to leave him if he didn't let the union organize. That was enough to make Henry give in, but not before serious losses in his own prestige and the loyalty of his employees.

The stubbornness exemplified in his policies toward the union was also evident in Henry's attitude toward the product. He would approve no major change in the Ford V-8, and had only reluctantly agreed to the Lincoln Zephyr. His company's lack of a broad product line began to show after 1935, the last year in the decade when Ford outproduced Chevrolet. The year 1938, a poor one for the entire industry, was particularly grim for Dearborn. That year's volume of 410,000 cars was only half the 1937 level. The Mercury didn't arrive until 1939, too late to help the company's fortunes. As a result, Fords of the late '30s were not the cars they might have been.

In 1938, the previous year's Deluxe body styling was applied to the standard model and the Deluxe was restyled. The Ford roadster had disappeared after 1937 and the phaeton would depart after 1938. Both of these body styles had long since lost whatever favor they once had, but Ford was far behind its competition in realizing this—Plymouth's last roadster and phaeton were built in 1932, Chevrolet's in 1935.

For 1938, the 60-bhp V-8 models were offered in three body styles: coupe, four-door sedan, and two-door sedan. The 85-bhp V-8s still came in standard and Deluxe lines offering a total of 11 body styles. The four-door convertible sedan priced at $900 was still top-of-the-line. The last rumble-seat body styles were also produced this year. Styling was a warmed over version of 1937: The grille/hood section became more bulbous, and standard models adopted the swept-back grille style.

The 1939 Ford Deluxe models were again fully restyled, and featured a vertical stainless steel grille and clean front fenders fitted with flush headlamps. Prices were reduced $5 on each model, and the convertible sedan put in its last appearance. Mechanical changes included column-mounted, instead of floor-mounted, gearshift and hydraulic, instead of mechanical, brakes. On the last point, Henry Ford had finally given in—three years after Chevrolet and 11 years after Plymouth.

People raced Ford V-8s from the day they appeared, and not without success. There was even a team of Ford-based Indianapolis racers, though V-8s were less successful at the 500 than in road racing. The attraction of the pretty Model A and the sleek, fast V-8 has persisted to the present. Today, Ford is the most popular marque by far among cars of the '30s.

Two major Model A organizations exist: the Model A Ford Club of America, Box 1791, Whittier, California 90603; and the Model A Restorers Club, Box 1930, Dearborn, Michigan 48124. The V-8s are celebrated by the Early Ford V-8 Club of America, Box 2122, San Leandro, California 94577.

Despite an enormous supply, some 1930s Fords are expensive today: $15,000 is not an unknown figure for a prize-winning V-8 convertible sedan. An equally large supply of original body and mechanical parts is available and some companies specialize in reproduction parts, so restorers should have no difficulty finding what they need. Vehicle authenticity down to the last detail is strongly emphasized in Ford club judging.

photo credits: *Ford Motor Company; Timmis Motor Co., Ltd.*

Franklin

Franklin Automobile Company, Syracuse, New York

Franklin was the only really successful air-cooled luxury car in America. Since 1902, Franklins had been built in the firm's Syracuse factory, and had always been known for high quality and innovation. Franklin engineers traditionally emphasized lightweight construction. For example, in the 1920s and '30s, when cast iron was considered the standard stuff of engine block, pistons, and cylinder head, Franklins used high-grade aluminum. Ever since Charles A. Lindbergh's air-cooled-engine monoplane made its trans-Atlantic flight in 1927, Franklin advertising writers had taken care to mention that this car was powered by a similarly cooled engine. Franklin even named its line of 1928 cars the "Airman" in honor of the Lone Eagle, and the company retained this name for one of its models right up until it ceased production in 1934.

Like most manufacturers, Franklin entered 1930 with an overly optimistic attitude towards the future. The firm had a banner sales year in 1929; interest in aviation and air-cooled engines was at its peak. The Series 14 Franklins for 1930 reflected the company's enthusiasm with new styling and a brand-new engine. The new series had a restyled radiator shell (which Franklin always called a "hood front"—a conventional-looking front end was considered essential for sales appeal). The shell had shutters which opened and closed to govern the amount of air entering the engine compartment. The shutter opening was automatically controlled by a thermostat, which ran according to the temperature of the number-one cylinder.

The supercharged air-cooled 1930 engine had six individually cast cylinders and overhead valves as in previous models, but unlike its predecessors, incoming air was directed to the sides of the cylinders from left to right. Thus, it became known as the "side-blast engine" among Franklin owners. Displacement was 274 cubic inches and horsepower was 95 bhp at 3100 rpm. Prices for the standard models were $2585-$2885.

Franklin had always been a luxury automobile and its chassis were the basis for many custom bodies by Derham, Dietrich, Locke, and Brunn. One of the more unusual 1930 body styles was the "Pirate," an open four-door convertible designed by Dietrich. It was available as either a five-passenger phaeton or a seven-passenger touring. Its most striking feature was its flared out doors and running boards completely covered by the lower body.

Also introduced in 1930 was the "Pursuit" dual-cowl phaeton which had no external door handles: They were eliminated to give the car cleaner lines. Upholstery in the driver's compartment wrapped up and over the outer edge of the doors, a feature which imitated the cockpits of aircraft from the period. Dietrich also

built a popular four-door four-passenger speedster with a shortened body that ended midway over the rear wheels. Most speedsters were closed cars with a permanent canvas top, but a full-convertible model was available at extra cost.

As you might guess, aviators and aviatrix of the era consistently chose Franklins: Charles Lindbergh, Amelia Earhart, and Frank Hawks were all Franklin owners. But, though Franklin had its sporty-looking models, it was never known as a flashy car. The major-

1930 Franklin Series 145 sport sedan

1930 Franklin "Pirate" touring by Dietrich

1930 Franklin Series 145 town car by Derham

Franklin

ity were purchased by professionals—doctors, attorneys, and business executives. The cars were painted in conservative colors and usually had blackwall tires. Franklin had pioneered closed-car construction and offered sedan models before 1920. So, Franklins may be described briefly as conservative, elegant, and expensive. Their owners were loyal and repeat customers.

Franklin reported that its share of what is termed the "fine car business" gained 100 percent in the first quarter of 1930, compared to the same period in 1928. But in fact, there was no fine car business. The great Depression had a death grip on the prestige market, and by the end of 1930, total sales had reached only 6043—less than half that of the record 1929 year. In an attempt to maintain previous production levels, Franklin introduced the Transcontinent model in May, 1930. This was the lowest-priced sedan Franklin ever offered at $2395, but it was still four times as costly as a new Model A Ford. In those days, remember, $2395 amounted to a very nice annual salary.

To prove that its engine was really airplane-like, Franklin made arrangements to install one in a Waco

biplane which flew, and well. Its pilot remarked that he was amazed at the engine's power. Coast-to-coast record driver E. G. "Cannonball" Baker echoed the pilot's praise. It was hard to imagine a nationally known endurance driver taking on all comers in a conservative Franklin sedan, but "Cannonball" did, and in the process, broke many long-established records. One was the New York-Miami run, which Baker completed at an average speed of 59.6 mph. And between Fort Myers and Miami, "Bake" averaged 75.6 mph—faster than the carded aircraft time.

For 1931, Franklin fielded a model lineup similar to 1930, but lower in price. The 125-inch wheelbase Transcontinent coupe, covertible, victoria brougham, and sedan listed for $1795-$1895. The larger Deluxes offered a speedster, convertible, victoria brougham, and sedan styles priced at $2295-$2695. Mounted on a 132-inch wheelbase, Deluxes were restyled and strikingly handsome, with more rakish clamshell fenders and flowing body lines designed by Ray Dietrich. Advertising continued to push the car's similarities to aircraft and featured cars in the foreground with airplane silhouettes in the background. Phrases such as "Riding like Gliding" dominated promotional material but the company's enthusiasm was countered by the gloom of the Depression. Sales for model year 1931

1931 Franklin Deluxe speedster four-passenger sedan by Dietrich

1931 Franklin Deluxe "Pirate" touring

1931 Franklin Series 15 Deluxe town car by Dietrich

CONSUMER GUIDE®

totaled only 2851 units.

In 1932, Franklin hatched a revolutionary idea: a supercharged air-cooled V-12. The engine displaced 398 cubic inches and developed 150 bhp. Initially, it was planned for the 132-inch-wheelbase Airman body and chassis. The engine was ready for 1931, but financial problems held up its introduction. Franklin had failed to meet payment on certain bank notes, and the banks sent in managers to protect their investment.

Franklin president Edwin McEwan, meanwhile, decided some changes were needed for the new Twelve, which accordingly bowed as an entirely new and larger car. The production Twelve resembled previous Franklins in engine only. Instead of the traditional full-elliptic springs and tubular front axle, the Twelve had semi-elliptics and an I-beam front axle. Instead of a body built by Franklin's long-time supplier, the Walker Co. of Massachusetts, the Twelve's bodies were hand-made at Franklin's Syracuse factory. LeBaron was responsible for the styling, which embodied an extended hood running back to a rakishly angled windshield, and a sharply vee'd "hood cover." By the standards of 1932, it was exotic.

Prices for the Franklin Twelve ran from $3885 to $4185, and the cars used a 144-inch wheelbase. Approximately 200 were built. The only body styles offered were sedans and a two-door club brougham. Despite their variation from traditional Franklin themes, the cars were magnificent to look at: Their size alone was overwhelming.

For 1932, the six-cylinder Airman continued to use Walker bodies, full-elliptic springs, and the 100-bhp, 274-cid engine. Counting the 200-odd Twelves, 1932 sales amounted to only 1905 units. Franklin's trail was now narrowing appreciably.

For 1933, Franklin introduced its lowest-priced model ever, the Olympic. This was the product of co-operation with Reo, another auto firm facing imminent demise, and was basically the Franklin engine married to the Reo Flying Cloud chassis, with Franklin supplying the finished product. Reo shipped 30 Flying Cloud bodies a day from its Lansing, Michigan factory to Syracuse. After a day on the production line, the cars would roll out as new Franklin Olympics. The tooling cost for the Reo-Olympic conversion was only $2500, and the retail price was attractive: $1385 for the coupe or sedan and $1500 for the convertible.

Olympics were very good cars, but they arrived too late to save the Franklin Automobile Company. The last years for the marque were 1933 and 1934, when registrations totaled only 1329 and 360 cars, respectively. A full line of Olympics, Airman Sixes, and Twelves was ostensibly offered in both years, but by April, 1934, the Franklin factory had closed its doors forever.

All 1930s Franklins, except for the Olympics, are recognized as Classics, which makes the Olympics as good a buy now as they were when new. A 1978 list of recorded prices shows a near-perfect condition 1933 Olympic coupe selling at $6490, a 1932 Airman sedan for $6900, and a 1933 Twelve sedan for $18,250.

1932 Franklin Series 16 seven-passenger sedan

1932 Franklin Deluxe convertible coupe

1933 Franklin Twelve five-passenger sedan

1933 Franklin Olympic four-door sedan

Prices in each case are inevitably going to rise, and it's questionable whether they are representative of the three basic types of '30s-era Franklins. Twelves may now command up to 50 percent more, for example, and open models are sure to be costlier than sedans.

If you end up with one, though, you'll have lots of good company. The H. H. Franklin Club, 197 Mayfair Avenue, Floral Park, New York 11001, welcomes all models.

photo credit: *Walt Gosden, Motor Vehicle Manufacturers Association*

Graham

Graham-Paige Motors Corporation, Detroit, Michigan

The 1930 Grahams comprised a variety of models in several body styles, all powered by L-head sixes and straight eights. The largest Eight, with 120 bhp, included among its 137-inch-wheelbase body styles a beautiful town car by LeBaron. Special Sixes and Eights and Custom Eights all featured Graham-Paige's famous four-speed transmission. Prices were around $1000-$1800 for the Sixes, and $2000 and up for the Eights, all the way to the LeBaron town car at $4480.

The same line continued through early 1932, with a mid-1931 introduction called the "Prosperity Six," a $785 price leader. But Graham-Paige failed to prosper. Sales in 1930 were 33,560, only half the 1929 total, and slid to 20,428 in 1931.

Graham dug in for 1932, offering a conventional six-cylinder car and the new Blue Streak Eight. The Blue Streak was a magnificent design by Amos Northup, who had also created the 1931 Reo Royale. Its then-novel skirted fenders would be a universal industry design touch a few years later. It used a 245.4-cid eight, had a 123-inch wheelbase and lots of special

1936 Graham Supercharger (Series 110) two-door sedan

1939 Graham Supercharged club sedan

features: a "banjo" frame, outboard springs, and an aluminum cylinder head. In good times it would have sold well, but 1932 was hardly a good year for anyone. Production was 12,967, and in 1933 it was down further to 10,970.

Graham fielded another fine car in 1934, the Supercharged Custom Eight. The blower, running at 23,000 rpm, boosted horsepower from 95 on the unblown versions to 135 bhp. At $1245, this was the first moderately priced supercharged American car, and through the next six years, Graham would build more supercharged models than any company before or since. Production rose to 15,745 for the 1934 model year.

The line was reworked in 1935, but was now quite ugly. Sales nevertheless improved to the 20,000-plus level, and would remain there for two more years. In 1936, the eights were dropped, but Graham-Paige now offered America's first supercharged six. With 217.8 cid and 112 to 120 bhp, this would be the company's basic engine through 1941. The two models offered were called Supercharger and Cavalier, and shared their Hayes-built bodies with the Reo Flying Cloud as a result of merger talks between the two auto makers during 1935. A combination was never created, though Graham used Reo bodies through 1937, which resulted in some very ordinary-looking models. The smaller 1936-37 Crusader was based on the 1935 design; its tooling was sold to Nissan of Japan (makers of the Datsun) in 1937.

There was nothing ordinary about the 1938 "Spirit of Motion" Grahams, with a sharply undercut front end that soon earned the nickname "sharknose." Again, Graham styling was far ahead, and again, the public did not respond. Production dropped to less than 5000 cars in 1938. In 1939, a sharknose two-door sedan and club coupe joined the sedan, but Grahams remained poor sellers. Amos Northup's last design before his death, the sharknose was taken out of production after 1940.

Also in 1940, Graham built the Cord-based Hollywood alongside the Hupp Skylark in its Dearborn plant, but that model also failed to stem the company's losses. By September, 1940, Graham was out of the car business.

Today, the only Grahams rated as Classics are the custom-bodied 1930 models by LeBaron or Erdmann & Rossi. Two organizations exist: the Graham Owners Club, Box 105, Burlington, Massachusetts 01803; and the Hupmobile-Graham Club, Box 215, Glenview, Illinois 60025. The latter is currently inactive, but will answer owner's questions.

photo credit: *Motor Vehicle Manufacturers Association*

Hudson, Essex & Terraplane

Hudson Motor Car Company, Detroit, Michigan

Proud old Hudson was founded back in 1908 and floundered for most of the 1930s. The Depression all but wiped out the market for the big Hudson, while the inexpensive little Essex seemed unable to sell even when the times were right for it. Essex had been a winner when it was introduced in 1922: It had a lively four-cylinder engine and was the first mass-produced popular-priced closed car. When Essex adopted a less reliable six in 1924, its reputation suffered accordingly. Though the engine was improved and enlarged in 1930 and 1931, Essex failed to win back its early reputation for ruggedness and reliability. So, the fortunes of Hudson fell first in the early '30s and again in the recession of 1938. The one high point of the decade fell right between those times and was achieved by Roy D. Chapin on the shoulders of the Terraplane.

Chapin—father of recent American Motors board chairman Roy D. Chapin, Jr.—was one of Hudson's founders. Later, he became Secretary of Commerce under President Hoover, but returned to Hudson when Hoover left office in the spring of 1933. Immediately, Chapin realized the Essex needed some major changes and fast. Its side-valve six had been increased to 160 cid and 58 bhp in 1930, then to 175.3 cid and 60 bhp in 1931—why not make it larger still? Accordingly, the engine was bored and stroked to 193 cubic inches, in which form it delivered 70 bhp.

The new engine was put into a model labeled the Essex "Greater Super Six" and was field-tested on the standard 113-inch-wheelbase in early 1932. In mid-1932, Chapin put it into a new 106-inch-wheelbase chassis and called the result Essex Terraplane. "In the air, it's aeroplaning," read the Hudson ads. "On the water, it's hydroplaning. On the ground, hot diggety dog, that's Terraplaning!"

The 1932-33 Essex Terraplane turned the company's fortunes around. And why not? It was fast—up to 80 mph; it was economical—up to 25 mpg; and it was cheap—as little as $425. In 1933, there was an eight-cylinder option, a 243.9-cid evolution of the Terraplane six. Terraplanes set numerous speed marks in the middle '30s including over 100 stock-car records. The public responded and by 1934, when the name Essex was dropped and Terraplane became a marque in its own right, production had moved up to 85,000 units, Hudson's best showing since 1930. The company was now in fifth place in the industry. (Also in 1934, the Terraplane Eight was dropped, but a new six of 212.1 cubic inches arrived. This was even more powerful: 80 bhp in 1934 and 88 bhp in 1935-37.) Terraplane became a Hudson series by 1938, and disappeared completely after 1939—but in the middle '30s, it literally saved the company.

While 1932 Essex Terraplanes had sold for as little as $425, most 1933 Terraplanes listed for around $500-$600. The sportier models cost more, of course. While Essex had been a boxy, bolt-upright car, the Terraplane's styling adopted sleek, streamlined features like a raked-back radiator grille and skirted fenders. A vast array of models and body styles was offered. Unlike most lower-priced cars of the period, the Terraplane was tastefully styled and avoided the excesses of the era, except for a debatable waterfall grille in 1936-37.

1930 Hudson Great Eight club sedan by LeBaron

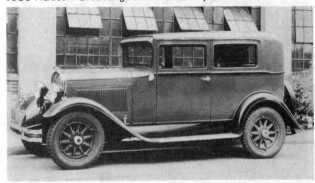

1931 Essex Super Six coach

1931 Hudson Great Eight sport roadster by Murray

Hudson, Essex & Terraplane

Although the Terraplane gradually grew from a 106-inch wheelbase in 1932 to 112/116 inches in 1934 and 115 inches in 1936-37, the cars remained good performers. An English road test of the 1936 model sedan recorded 0 to 60 mph in 26.6 seconds and a top speed of 82 mph—highly creditable at the time for a car that weighed 2770 pounds. "The six-cylinder engine gives plenty of power and has that suppleness and quietness in its running that are characteristic of American de-

1932 Essex Terraplane four-door sedan (driven by Amelia Earhart)

1933 Essex Terraplane Eight convertible coupe (with Roy D. Chapin, Sr.)

1933 Hudson Super Six two-passenger coupe

sign," wrote the editors. "The speed at which this car travels on the open road is almost wholly a matter of the driver's choice . . . Even at 70 there is no special fuss from the mechanism. It can thus be a decidedly swift car for journeying over long distances, and is an easy one to handle, too . . . The Terraplane gives, and does, much for its price." Today's collectors agree: Terraplanes are among the most desirable Hudson products of the 1930s.

The big Hudson had forged its reputation during the '20s with the Super and Special Sixes—big-engined, smooth-looking, solidly built cars that offered a lot of performance for the money. In 1930, however, Hudson switched to what it called the Great Eight, an engine which, at 213.8 cid, was actually smaller than the previous sixes. The Great Eight produced only 80 bhp to power the car's heavy 119/126-inch-wheelbase chassis. The engine had an integrally cast block and crankcase, and the first counterweighted crankshaft ever designed for a straight eight. But its splash lubrication system was of outmoded design.

Hudson stayed with this engine for several years. For 1931, engineers bored it out to 233.7 cid, achieving 87 horsepower; in 1932, they bored it again to obtain 254.5 cubic inches and 101 horsepower. The engine remained at this displacement through the end of the decade though horsepower rose to as much as 128 bhp with an optional high-compression aluminum cylinder head.

Sadly, for Hudson, 1930 saw the closure of the Biddle and Smart Coachworks, which had provided magnificent open bodies for the firm in previous years (the only Hudsons rated as Classics by the CCCA). The company placed some orders for phaeton and speedster bodies with Murray and Briggs in the early '30s, and a few eight-cylinder chassis had dashing LeBaron coachwork. Through 1933 (the last year for the classic four-square Hudson styling), numerous body styles were offered on wheelbases from 119 to 133 inches. Roadsters, victorias, convertibles, sedans, town sedans, coupes, and broughams appeared. It was an attractive line of bodies which would have done justice to many more expensive chassis. Yet Hudson prices were as low as $995; the highest-priced model in this period was the $1350 "Major" seven-passenger sedan for 1933.

Six-cylinder Hudsons did not appear in 1930-32 because all the company's sixes were in the Essex line. In retrospect, this seems to have been a mistake. Not only did Hudson sixes have a flawless reputation, but the general economy would have been conducive to sales. To fill the void, the company launched a new Hudson Super Six in 1933. Essentially, this was the 193-cid Terraplane engine in the 113-inch-wheelbase Hudson chassis. The Super Six sold for about $700-$800, and six models were offered: runabout, phaeton, two coupes, and two sedans. But this was the bottom of the Depression for the firm and sales of all Hudson models were few. For 1934, Hudson again put all its sixes into its junior make, the Terraplane.

Along with just about everybody else, Hudson em-

1936 Hudson Eight four-door touring sedan

1936 Hudson Eight four-door sedan

1937 Hudson Eight convertible brougham

braced streamlining in the mid-30s as the old classic look, with its roots in Greek architecture, gradually gave way to the new style. Hudsons of 1934-35 were transitional designs, still basically boxes, but less upright than before. For 1936, styling was all new and could be compared to the Chrysler and DeSoto Airstreams of a year earlier—not quite Airflow-radical, but a lot more slippery-looking than before. The '36s had skirted fenders, and their rear wheel openings were often covered. They also had tall, rounded, Plymouth-like die-cast grilles and dowdy all-steel bodies.

Perhaps this move toward the popular "potato shape" came a bit late for Hudson, as suggested by its decreased market share during 1935-36. While 85,000 units had earned Hudson fifth place in production during 1934, over 100,000 units annually was good for only eighth place during 1935-37. There is also evidence the company was cutting prices beyond the point of being able to make adequate profits as Hudson continued to lose money despite doubled production volume in 1934. In 1934 and 1937, it made less than $1 million profit; with the 1938 recession, Hudson lost close to $5 million. This trend continued until 1941, when defense work helped the company recover. But

when car production ended in 1942, Hudson was one of the weaker surviving independents.

In 1935, the big Hudson lineup again included a six-cylinder series. This time it rode a 116-inch wheelbase, but as in '33, it used the Terraplane engine, now at 212.1 cid. In the large cars this engine delivered 93 bhp, a bit more than in the Terraplanes. The 212 engine was continued through the rest of the decade on cars using wheelbases as long as 122 inches.

By 1938, and in the face of that year's economic downturn, Roy D. Chapin reversed his emphasis on performance and concentrated on economy. The Terraplane became a Hudson model that year (only to vanish the next year) and was joined by the all-new Hudson 112 (named for its wheelbase). It had a small six of 190.8 cubic inches, which developed 86 bhp at 4000 rpm. The 112 was diametrically the opposite of a Terraplane: 0-60 mph took 35 seconds and its top speed was barely 70 mph. But, it did return up to 24 miles per gallon, and prices were as low as $694. The Deluxe convertible brougham cost less than $900.

In 1939, the 112 was reduced to a single Deluxe line. Now that the economy was looking up again, Hudson launched the 118-inch-wheelbase Pacemaker and the

Hudson, Essex & Terraplane

122-inch-wheelbase Country Club. Both these models used the Terraplane's 212.1-cid engine. A special series for 1939 was the Big Boy, riding a 119-inch wheelbase. Big Boys were large, comfortable closed cars and were available in just two models: a sedan using the 190.8-cid six, and a seven-passenger sedan with the 212.1-cid six. These cars were priced at $884 and $1114, respectively. The 1939 lineup also included a Country Club Eight, on 122- and 129-inch wheelbases.

The 1939 model year marked the last appearance of the bulky Hudson body introduced in 1936, but the '39 version was probably the best. The long-wheelbase models were especially graceful. Thick, horizontal grille bars gave them a cleaner frontal appearance than the controversial waterfall grille of 1937-38. In 1940, Hudsons would be fully redesigned, gaining a less distinctive look which closely resembled contemporary Ford products.

Despite the company's mixed fortunes in this decade, the 1930s offer good pickings for the Hudson collector. As with many other popular makes, the ultra-classic 1930-31 models are the most highly sought-after. Since Hudson did not adopt total streamlining until 1936, its 1932-35 models are also appealing to collectors who admire more upright lines. The Terraplane—particularly the 106-inch wheelbase model—is a fine performing car, and its styling in 1933-34 is hard to fault. The most coveted Hudsons of the decade are the Eights, especially the custom-bodied open models, even though they're among the most expensive Hudsons on today's market. All Hudson products are welcomed by an excellent organization, the 4000-member Hudson-Essex-Terraplane Club, 100 East Cross Street, Ypsilanti, Michigan 48197.

photo credit: *American Motors Corporation*

1938 Hudson Eight touring sedan

1939 Hudson 112 four-door touring sedan

1939 Hudson Six coupe

Hupmobile

Hupp Motor Car Corporation
Detroit, Michigan and Cleveland, Ohio

Hupp began the 1930s after two record sales years, and watched production plunge to 22,183 in the first year of the new decade. The 1930 Hupmobile line was comprised of the six-cylinder Model S, assembled in the Cleveland plant formerly used by Chandler, and three Detroit-built straight-eight cars, the Models C, H, and U. The S and C were the firm's bread-and-butter cars and used a 211.6-cid six and a 268.8-cid eight, respectively. The H and U had a big 365.6-cid eight and included some luxurious limousines on a 137-inch wheelbase.

The next year saw more of the same, plus the new Model L Century with its 240.2-cid straight eight. The Series U included one of the handsomest Hupmobiles ever, a two-door victoria on a 137-inch wheelbase. Free-wheeling was featured this year. Hupp flew buyers to Detroit and Cleveland to stimulate sales, but in spite of this, production remained low, totaling 17,451 for the 1931 model year.

Beginning in 1932, Hupp used a code to designate year and wheelbase. The B-216, for example, was a 116-inch wheelbase six. This was also the year Hupp acquired the services of designer Raymond Loewy, who styled the F-222 and I-226 eight-cylinder models. Loewy's graceful bodies sported tire-hugging cycle-type fenders. They were handsome cars, with vee'd radiator grilles, sloping windshields, and chrome disc wheels. Though the Loewy designs won many styling awards, Hupmobile production dropped again to 10,647 for the model year.

Sales were the worst yet in 1933—just 7316 units. Essentially, the '33 was a carryover model, a sloping grille being the major change. A new cycle-fender six-cylinder model, the K-321, was followed by a cheap model, the K-321A. The latter was priced $100 less than the K-321, had a single windshield wiper and taillight, and stationary hood louvers. It didn't contribute to sales.

In 1934, Hupp released the radical Loewy-designed 421-J and 427-T, a six and an eight, respectively. Called the Aerodynamics, these cars had three-piece wrapped windshields, faired-in headlights and flush-mounted spare tires on their decks. The conventional 417-W six was also available, using Ford body parts. Sales rose to 9420. The '34s were largely unchanged for 1935, but were joined by the smaller Series 518-D Aerodynamic six with flat windshield, and the 121-inch-wheelbase eight-cylinder Model L.

The big news in this period was the fight for control of the company. The promoter of the Ruxton front-drive car, Archie Andrews, had gained control of Hupp in late 1934. By the time he was forced out a year later, the firm was in ruins. Hupp closed in early 1936 and stayed closed for over 18 months.

In 1938, the company came back with the conven-

tional 822-E six and 825-H eight. Hupp returned just in time for the 1938 recession, and built just 1752 cars. For 1939, the '38s were continued along with the new Hupmobile Skylark. This had a sedan body derived from the Cord 812 Beverly/Winchester. Hupp was deluged with orders, but couldn't get the Skylark into production. Just 35 hand-built prototype Skylarks were built, along with 1900 big cars. In 1940-41, Hupp merged production with Graham at the latter's Dearborn plant, but only 354 Skylarks could be built before Hupp gave up on cars in July, 1940.

Fans of the marque may be interested in joining the Hupmobile Club, Box AA, Rosemead, California 91770.

photo credit: *Motor Vehicle Manufacturers Association*

1934 Hupmobile Eight "Aerodynamic" sedan

1939 Hupmobile Skylark sedan (model R-915)

Lincoln
Lincoln Motor Company, Detroit, Michigan

Lincoln and Cadillac had a common founder—the stern, patrician Henry Martyn Leland, sometimes called the "Master of Precision." Cadillac entered the 1930s with its prestigious, modern Sixteen, but Lincoln had only its obsolete Model L chassis, created by Leland ten years before. Leland had sold out to Ford Motor Company when Lincoln hit financial trouble in 1922, and little had been done since then to alter his original design. Leland's engine was a V-8 of 385 cubic inches, but it produced only 90 horsepower. The 1930 Model L was therefore an anachronism: beautifully built, lavishly furnished, yet unfashionably upright and quite slow compared to the Cadillacs, Packards, and Chrysler Imperials. Ford, however, had a better idea coming.

For 1931, Lincoln announced the new Model K. (Exactly why the model designations went backwards remains a mystery.) With a modernized Model L V-8 and a massive new chassis, the K served as a bridge between Lincoln designs of the 1920s and '30s. Its engine had the Model L's bore-and-stroke dimensions, "fork-and-blade" rods, and three-piece block and crankcase assembly in cast iron. These "Leland touches" allowed Ford ads to dwell lovingly on the "precision-built Lincoln."

But the '31 K chassis was really designed for an all-new V-12 engine scheduled to arrive in 1932. Against 1930's 136-inch wheelbase, the K's measured 145 inches. The frame was nine inches deep and had six cross-members with cruciform bracing. Like the L, the K had torque-tube drive and floating rear axle. Steering was by worm-and-roller, hydraulic shocks were by Houdaille, and mechanical brakes by Bendix. The K's slightly peaked radiator lead a hood far longer than the L's, punctuated by twin trumpet horns and bowl-shaped headlamps. Compared to the L, the K was longer, lower, and sleeker. It offered an improved ride, greater stability, and more power (120 bhp at 2800 rpm) with faster acceleration and a higher top speed.

The 12-cylinder Model KB of 1932 was Lincoln's answer to the multi-cylinder challenges from Cadillac, Packard, and others. The 448 cubic-inch V-12 developed 150 bhp at 3400 rpm, providing still better perfor-

1931 Lincoln Model K sedan by LeBaron

1932 Lincoln KA limousine by Murray

1932 Lincoln KB convertible sedan by Waterhouse

mance than the Model K's V-8. Yet, the KB sold for slightly less than its predecessor—The LeBaron roadster, for example, was priced at $4700 as a '31 Model K and $4600 as a '32 KB. A wide range of bodies was offered for the KB: LeBaron roadster, Murphy sports roadster, Dietrich coupes and convertible sedan, Judkins berline, Brunn cabriolet and brougham, Willoughby panel brougham and limousine, plus numerous factory styles. A magnificent town car and an extremely fast tourer, the Lincoln KB was an extraordinary machine. It stood far above the general level of cars in its day, with performance as impressive as its appearance.

Alongside the 1932 KB, Lincoln continued the V-8 model on a 136-inch-wheelbase chassis and designated the KA. Though this chassis was dimensionally the same as the old Model L's, it was mechanically equal to the KB's. The V-8 was stepped up to 125 bhp, and a line of Murray bodies in ten styles was offered at prices which started at $2900. The bodies were simply furnished, but the car was a high-class concept, not a middle-priced product. Even so, the KA V-8 was not as smooth as the Cadillac, Packard or Pierce-Arrow eights. Its successor arrived in 1933 in the form of another Lincoln V-12.

The new "small" V-12 engine displaced 381.7 cubic inches and had horsepower equal to that of the KA V-8. It was installed in the 136-inch-wheelbase chassis with

1933 Lincoln KB five-passenger berline by Judkins

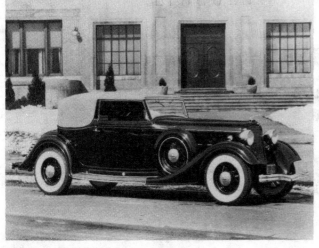

1934 Lincoln KV-12 convertible coupe

Murray-built wood, steel, and aluminum bodies. The KB, meanwhile, continued in 1933 as the senior Lincoln. There was also a new front-end appearance that year featuring a rakish vee'd radiator shell with a chrome grille concealing vertical shutters. Hoods were louvered instead of shuttered, and fenders were skirted. The front bumper was vee'd and the trunk rack was redesigned.

In 1934, Lincoln merged the KA and KB into one series, but the two distinct wheelbases were retained. The car was now known simply as the K V-12 and used a bored-out version of the 1933 Model KA engine with 414 cubic inches and 150 bhp. Its aluminum cylinder head gave a 6.38:1 compression ratio which was unheard of at the time. This was made possible by the newly available 70-octane Ethyl gas—and in 1934, 70-octane was almost the rating of aviation fuel. The '34 Lincoln had a top speed of about 95 mph, and was capable of higher rpm than the previous KB V-12. The chassis was virtually unchanged from 1933. Its radiator, however, was lacquered in body color. Smaller headlamps and parking lamps and metal spare tire covers were fitted and the Murray custom bodies were eliminated.

Lincoln sedans and limousines had sloping tails in 1934—a fairly radical departure from contemporary styling norms. Like Pierce, Packard, and Stutz, however, Lincoln was reluctant to change the graceful sweep of the "ogee curve" fenders which so indelibly marked the classic era. Those fenders were untouched for 1934 and 1935.

However, in 1936, there were semi-teardrop fenders, along with a simplifed radiator grille, new disc wheels, and larger hubcaps. In 1937, styling emphasized absolute simplicity—possibly the result of Cord 810 influence. Headlamps were now integral with the fenders, belt moldings were eliminated, and doors were extended almost to the running boards. The spare tire was enclosed in the trunk unless side-mount spares were specified. For the first time on a standard Lincoln, a V-shaped windshield was used. The standard interior was done in rich broadcloth with curly-maple garnish moldings. Rarer woods and fabrics were available on custom models. Prices for the four-door sedan in 1937 were $4400 and $4700 for the136- and 145-inch wheelbases, respectively.

The 1937 Model K had its engine moved further forward, which improved the ride, and the engine had hydraulic tappets for the first time. Output was still 150 bhp, but '37 and later models are thought to have had more power than previous Ks because of a different cam contour. Synchromesh transmission also arrived in 1937. In other respects, the chassis was much the same as before. Prices for four-door sedans, which remained unchanged from 1938 through the final 1940 models, were $4900 and $5000 for the 136- and 145-inch-wheelbase versions, respectively.

The Lincoln market, which had been so strong in the '20s, dried up like an Arizona creek bed in the economic drought of the '30s. Lincoln's near-9000 unit sales in 1926 was not equalled until 1935; the best

Lincoln

interim total was 5311 in 1931. After 1934, Lincoln never produced more than 2000 Model Ks a year. In fact, the 1940 models were available only to special order, and actually used chassis built during 1939. (The largest of these, the 160-inch-wheelbase "Sunshine Special," was the parade car of Presidents Roosevelt and Truman, and may be seen today at the Henry Ford Museum in Dearborn, Michigan.)

The result of all this was that, like Cadillac and Packard, Lincoln was forced to develop a high-volume product for the decade of austerity. This was introduced for the 1936 model year as the Lincoln Zephyr. The Zephyr's radical unit body was designed by John Tjaarda using aircraft construction principles. It was also a genuinely slippery shape. Tjaarda's prototype was built with the help of the Briggs Body Company, which was anxious to get some volume business out of Lincoln at last.

Tjaarda's body was initially intended to have a rear-mounted engine, but Ford ultimately decided to go with the conventional front-engine layout. The rest of the package was unconventional enough, however. According to Tjaarda, the Zephyr was the first car in which aircraft-type stress analysis actually proved the structural advantage of unit body construction. With a curb weight of 3300 pounds, the Zephyr was lighter than the Chrysler Airflow, yet it was much stiffer. In crash tests, its body resisted nearly twice the impact conventionally built bodies could sustain. Best of all, it was a lot cheaper to manufacture than a separate body and chassis.

Ford had hoped to power the lightweight Zephyr with a modified Ford V-8 producing 100 bhp, but Edsel Ford decided this would be inadequate. Therefore, Lincoln engineer Frank Johnson was directed to produce a V-12 engine derived from the Ford V-8. Johnson was one of the ablest engineers in the industry, but because of the project's limitations, this engine did not turn out to be an outstanding one. An L-head V-12 with four main bearings, it was a unit block casting with an exhaust cored between the cylinders. Thus, it was more like a "12-cylinder Ford V-8" than a true Lincoln engine. It displaced 267 cubic inches and developed 100 bhp, which was hardly earthshaking. The rest of the Zephyr drivetrain was also derived from the Ford V-8 and the car's wheelbase was 122 inches.

Styling was similar to Tjaarda's early prototypes, but a raised hoodline and radiator intake were grafted on by Ford stylist E. T. "Bob" Gregorie. The Briggs Company actually built most of the Zephyr—Ford only did the final assembly by installing the drivetrain, adding the hood and fenders, and trimming and painting the cars. Edsel Ford laughingly told Tjaarda that he might as well let Briggs build the whole car since Ford's Zephyr assembly line was only 40 feet long!

The Lincoln Zephyr was announced in November,

1936 Lincoln KV-12 five-passenger sedan

1935 Lincoln KV-12 limousine by Judkins

1937 Lincoln KV-12 touring cabriolet by Brunn

1939 Lincoln KV-12 five-passenger cabriolet by Brunn

1935 in two body styles: a two-door and four-door sedan, priced respectively at $1275 and $1320. While it was intended to compete with the Packard One-Twenty and Cadillac's LaSalle, it was far closer in concept to the spectacularly unsuccessful Chrysler Airflow. Still, Zephyrs sold in numbers previously unheard of at Lincoln: 17,715 cars for model year 1936 and 25,243 units for 1937. Like all Lincolns and most Fords, the car was a good performer. Its top-end speed was over 87 mph, though with a 4.33 rear axle ratio it was geared more for acceleration than high speed. It would do 0-50 mph in 10.8 seconds and 30-50 mph in six seconds flat, yet consistently averaged 16 to 18 miles per gallon.

The whole Zephyr concept caused a great deal of interest in Europe. Tjaarda mentions Porsche, Mathis, Rasmassen (Auto Union), and Dolfous (Hispano-Suiza) as men interested in the design. The one most influenced, of course, was Dr. Porsche. Although it is never mentioned in Porsche biographies, the shape, and to some extent the construction, of the car that would become the Volkswagen was substantially the same as the first experimental rear-engine Zephyr.

The 1936 Zephyr was designated the Model H and continued with little change as the 1937 series HB. A coupe and town sedan were added that year, and the coupe sold for only $1165. For 1938, wheelbase was increased to 125 inches and the Zephyr was extensively restyled. An innovation was its "mouth organ" grille, with which Lincoln beat everyone to the next styling plateau. The Zephyr not only set the style for both Ford and Mercury in 1939, but several rival manufacturers including Hudson, Nash, and Studebaker, followed by other American makes.

Like so many other automotive developments, this grille involved both a revolution and an evolution. In the 1938 rendition, the grille was changed radically from a vertical to a more horizontal configuration. Then came evolutions over several years, and finally the "fix" of the modern form. Emphasis was now on the horizontal "mouth" instead of the vertical "nose." This was perhaps the most important styling change between the 1930s and the 1940s—and it all started with the '38 Lincoln Zephyr.

The restyled '38 was accompanied by an expanded model lineup. New were a convertible coupe and convertible sedan priced at $1700 and $1790. The range of closed cars continued at $1296 to $1550. The line was expanded to nine models in 1939, and although none of the styles were new, there were now standard and Custom interior options for many of them. Prices remained much as they'd been in 1938: from $1358 for the standard three-passenger coupe to $1839 for the convertible sedan.

The vast majority of Zephyrs were, of course, closed cars. Collectors are naturally interested in the rarer, sportier styles which were built in very small numbers. For the 1938/39 model years, respectively, production figures for these body types are: 130/150 town limousines, 461/302 convertible sedans, 600/640 convertible coupes, and 800/800 coupe-sedans.

1939 Lincoln Zephyr four-door sedan

1939 Lincoln Zephyr two-door sedan

Mechanical details of the late '30s Zephyr followed typical Ford practice, except for some exclusive Lincoln design features. Hydraulic brakes—because of Henry Ford's stubbornness—did not become available until 1939. In 1938, the V-12 received hydraulic tappets; post-1939 engines were larger and more powerful. A two-speed Columbia rear axle was optional and gave a 28 percent reduction in engine speed in its higher cruising ratio.

For collectors, the Lincoln Models L, K, KA, and KB are recognized as Classics, and have a devoted following in the Lincoln Owners Club, Box 189, Algonquin, Illinois 60102. The Zephyrs also have a following: the Lincoln Zephyr Owners Club, Box 185, Middletown, Pennsylvania 17057.

Classic Lincolns have long since run well into the five-figure prices, though once in a great while you might find a Model KA in reasonable condition for less than that, and very occasionally, a closed KB or Model L. Open Zephyrs are moving up fast in collector circles, though they will never sell for Model K prices. Among Zephyrs, the '38 is significant for its influential styling and the '36 for being first of the breed. Among Ks of the later years, rarity is a governing factor in value. Model year production was only 986 in 1937, 470 in 1938, and 120 in 1939-40.

photo credits: *Ford Archives; Ford Motor Company*

Marmon & Roosevelt

Marmon Motor Car Co.,
Indianapolis, Indiana

Anybody who could invent an air-cooled V-4 engine with overhead valves and pressure lubrication in 1902 had to be a genius, and Howard Marmon was certainly that. In the economic downturn following World War I, sales of Marmon's cars started faltering, and in 1924, George M. Williams was hired to put profitability back in the firm. Howard Marmon became board chairman, but didn't care for Williams' humdrum straight eights, and withdrew almost completely from corporate activities about 1926. He set up a branch company named Midwest Aircraft, and devoted himself to research. The Marmon Eights which followed, and continued on into the '30s are, therefore, the work of others.

Williams wanted Marmon to be a little General Motors offering nothing but straight eights, and new examples of that type engine were introduced almost yearly. The peak of activity was 1930: There was a facelifted Marmon-Roosevelt, revised versions of the earlier straight-eight cars named Models 69 and 79, and a luxurious Big Eight with 315 cid and 125 bhp. The price range now stretched from $1000 to $5000—Marmon was going all out. The expansion was too soon and too rapid, however, and Marmon's public image became confused. The Roosevelt (named for President Teddy) failed to make an impression in the lower-price field and it undermined the fine-car image of the big Marmons. From 22,300 cars in 1929, Marmon production sank to 12,300 units in 1930, 5768 in 1931, and 1365 cars in 1932.

In 1931, however, Howard Marmon's five years of research would culminate with the introduction of a brand new idea: the magnificent Marmon Sixteen. This mighty Classic packed 200 bhp from an engine of almost 500 cubic inches. It would do 100 mph and was priced at $5200-$5400. Unfortunately, Cadillac had introduced its own Sixteen a year earlier, and was already draining away what market existed for such extraordinary machines.

Marmon's V-16 layout comprised pushrod-operated overhead valves actuated by a single camshaft. The aluminum cylinders were a triumph of the foundry man's art. Both block and crankcase were cast as one unit, the block actually being a "Y" in section. One dual-throat downdraft carburetor fed the fuel, and a single cast manifold served both banks of cylinders. Though the engine displaced 491 cubic inches, its weight was a comparatively low 930 pounds complete with all accessories. This was some 370 pounds lighter than the contemporary Cadillac V-16. The Marmon's low weight-to-power ratio—4.65 pounds per horsepower—was probably rivalled only by Duesenberg.

Light alloy construction was also used for the rest of the car: The hood, front and rear splash aprons, running board aprons, spare wheel mounts, headlight and taillight brackets, and fuel filler pipe were all made of aluminum. Because of the Marmon's light weight, few cars could approach the Sixteen's sheer speed or acceleration through the gears. Its pick-up was superior even to the Duesenberg's, though the Duesie would win going away at higher speeds due to its double-overhead-cam engine design and superior breathing. Marmon enhanced its image by guaranteeing each Sixteen purchaser that his or her car had exceeded 100 mph for two complete laps of the Indy race track.

Body design of Marmon's greatest car caused as much interest as its engine. Although the body was not Howard Marmon's design, he must be credited with hiring an industrial designer to create it at a time when that profession was in its infancy. The designer was 47-year-old Walter Dorwin Teague Sr., but as he himself admitted, much of the work was done by his son. W. D. Teague Jr. made all the original sketches and drawings for the Sixteen's body, the full-sized renderings, and some interior designs (including the unusual aircraft-type instrument panel). The junior Teague was a student at MIT at the time and did the work in summer school and on weekends. Since his father's name had considerable prestige, Marmon publicity gave credit to Teague Sr. Indeed, the elder Teague handled the contract work with Marmon, and translated the Sixteen concept into the eventual production car.

With no resemblance to any previous Marmon, the Sixteen looked sensationally new. The raked "V" radiator grille was devoid of ornament or badge. The filler cap was under the hood, as was the fuel tank filler cap. The doors extended almost to the running boards. Fender flanges hid shock absorbers and steering connections. The beltline ran absolutely straight around the entire body. Windshield rake matched that of the radiator, and the roofline was ultra low. Unified in form, the Sixteen was described as a new concept in fine cars, in which engineering and body design were of equal importance.

A limited range of Sixteen standard bodies was built by LeBaron: five sedans, two coupes, and a victoria. Few custom bodies are known. Waterhouse built two tourers, but the most individual custom was a one-off victoria designed by Alexis de Sakhnoffsky and built by Hayes. The Sakhnoffsky victorias sold for a towering $5700, while the standard '31 Marmons ran from $5220 to $5400. (In 1932, though, the price of the standard bodies rose to $5700-$5900.)

Aside from the Sixteen, Marmon produced five different 1931 eights in two series. The first series began in August, 1930, and comprised the 113-inch wheelbase Roosevelt (201.9 cid/77 bhp), the 114-inch wheelbase Marmon 69 (211.2 cid/84 bhp), and the 136-inch wheelbase Big Eight (315.2 cid/125 bhp). The Big Eight was retained in the second production

1930 Marmon-Roosevelt

1932 Marmon V-16 all-weather phaeton

1932 Marmon V-16 touring sedan

series, which began in January, 1931, when it was called the Marmon 88. Compared to the Big Eight, the 88 was priced about $450 lower to spark sales. Another second-series 1931 eight was the Model 70, which replaced both the Roosevelt and the 69. It used the Roosevelt's chassis and the 69's engine, but it sold for around $900-$1000, about the same as the Roosevelt.

Despite this attempt to pare down its offerings to the most popular models, Marmon's sales picture was far from encouraging in 1931. With production down to around half of what it had been in 1930, Marmon stood 25th in the production race, between Reo and LaSalle. The Sixteen suffered a sales handicap right from the beginning because of a long delay between its announcement and the start of production. Prototypes were displayed at the winter 1930-31 auto shows, but the first buyer didn't take delivery of a Sixteen until April, 1931. Many buyers refused to wait and went elsewhere, frequently to Cadillac. Many other luxury-car prospects had, of course, gone into hiding. Those

people bought unobtrusive Fords, or at most, Chryslers. In September, 1931, Marmon announced 32 custom body designs for the Sixteen—town cars, all-weather models, limousines, sports models, and various sedans with sunshine roofs. This move came too late, and it's doubtful that any were built. For every Sixteen that Marmon made, Cadillac built ten of its comparable V-16s.

Along with declining sales, Marmon suffered from contradictory internal policies in the early '30s. The engineering department was divided into two warring camps; the production men had trouble getting Sixteens delivered; the sales force was harassed by the low-bucks image of the Roosevelt. For 1932, Marmon fielded only three models: the Sixteen, the eight-cylinder Model 70, and a 315.2-cid eight-cylinder car now known by its wheelbase measurement, the 125. Compared to the 1932 88, the 125 gave away nothing in engine specification, but its wheelbase had shrunk by up to 11 inches. Its price was shrunk, too: The sedan and coupe listed for just $1420 each, against $2275-$2220 for the comparable 88 models the year before.

Price and model cuts in the eight-cylinder ranges created a feeling among buyers that Marmon was abandoning the fine car field in 1932. Actually, the company was preparing to do just the opposite: In 1933, the Sixteen was the only car listed. Its price was cut by almost $1000 from the 1932 figure. The coupe and sedan sold for $4825, the seven-passenger sedan cost $4975, and the convertible sedan was offered at $5075. There were no changes in engine specifications, but sales were now down to a trickle.

Engineering brilliance, it should be noted, was not effective medicine for any car company in the depths of the Depression. The makes that survived did so on corporate strength and a strong market base, neither of which Marmon had.

An attempt was made in January, 1934, to revive the Sixteen when Marmon's assets were taken over by the American Automotive Corporation, organized and backed by Harry Miller and Preston Tucker. This effort failed, and the assets were finally liquidated by the receivers in 1937. Prior to receivership, Howard Marmon and chassis engineer George Freers had new designs on the board. One was a revolutionary V-12 car, a cut-down version of the V-16, with independent suspension, tubular "backbone" frame, aluminum body, and three-point chassis attachment. Its styling was by Teague: slab sides with pontoon fenders, built-in headlights, and integral trunk. The money for this prototype came from Howard Marmon's personal fortune, as his company had nothing, and totaled $160,000. Howard lost the lot. There was no chance for production, and the car was stored on Marmon's North Carolina estate until his death in 1943. It has since made its way to industrial designer Brooks Stevens' automotive museum in Mequon, Wisconsin.

photo credits: *Motor Vehicle Manufacturers Association*

Mercury

**Ford Motor Company,
Dearborn, Michigan**

New models introduced by Ford Motor Company in the '30s and early '40s were largely the product of Edsel Ford, Henry's perceptive son. Edsel's influence resulted in the Lincoln Zephyr of 1936, the Continental of 1940, and the Mercury of 1939. In price, Mercury was designed to fill a market gap between the Zephyr ($1350-$1800) and the Ford Deluxe ($650-$900), so its average price was pitched at around $1000. For 1939, four body styles were listed. Besides a four-door sedan, two-door sedan, coupe-sedan, and convertible coupe, a Mercury four-door convertible sedan was also built, but probably didn't see more than a handful of copies. This body style was part of the Mercury line in 1940 also, but was abandoned after 1941.

The '39 Mercury rode a 116-inch wheelbase, against 112 inches for Ford and 125 for the Lincoln Zephyr. Its styling was closely derived from the '39 Ford, the main difference being that the Mercury's grille was horizontal and the Ford's vertical, although the longer wheelbase gave the Mercury better proportions than the Ford. Its 239 cubic-inch flathead V-8, slightly larger than Ford's, produced 95 horsepower at 3600 rpm. Like other Ford products of 1939, Mercury featured new four-wheel hydraulic brakes. The Zephyr inspired Mercury's torque-tube rear axle arrangement.

Mercury sold 76,198 cars in model year 1939, and the make soon developed a performance image. With a 3.54:1 rear axle ratio, a Mercury would hit close to 95 mph right off the showroom floor. It would do the standing quarter-mile in a creditable 18.5 seconds, and at 60 mph the engine was turning only 2550 rpm. Driver controls, resting flush in the instrument panel, were easy to master. The dash itself was a fairly basic affair, with a central panel flanked by a glovebox on the right and instruments on the left. The instruments included a battery meter, trip odometer, and clock as well as the speedometer and the usual dials for amperes, oil pressure, water temperature, and fuel level.

Ford considered over 100 names for this new car, though it was hard to fault the aura of speed and performance suggested by the one chosen. Among the also-rans were a number of names which have since become familiar: Comet, Consul, Dart, Eagle, Falcon, Horizon, Rambler, and Valiant. The problem of finding original product names is not a new one in the Motor City.

photo credits: *Ford Archives*

1939 Mercury convertible coupe

1939 Mercury two-door sedan

1939 Mercury two-door coupe-sedan

1939 Mercury four-door sedan

CONSUMER GUIDE®

Nash & LaFayette

Nash Motors & Nash-Kelvinator,
Kenosha, Wisconsin

In 1916, crusty Charlie Nash tired of working for a boss at General Motors (he was president, but William C. Durant was chairman), and decided to build cars under his own name. That same year he bought the Thomas B. Jeffery Company in Kenosha, Wisconsin, which manufactured the low-selling Jeffery, and had earlier built a car called the Rambler. Nash lit a small fire under the firm, now called Nash Motors, and charged up to eighth place in production by 1921, literally from nowhere. In the heady 1920s, Nash bought LaFayette, which had produced a luxurious V-8 car, and also introduced the low-cost Ajax. Neither of these proved as successful as the Nash itself, and both were gone by the start of the '30s. Although Charles Nash brought out a new, much cheaper LaFayette in 1934, it survived as a distinct make only until 1936. Throughout the '30s, the company suffered from the general economic malaise. Nash recouped his losses in 1937 by merging with the Kelvinator appliance company, appointing cigar-chomping George Mason as president; Nash himself remained chairman. By 1940, the firm had turned the corner and was profitable.

Nashes of the early '30s were beautiful and quite sumptuous automobiles with lots of special features. A very ordinary side-valve six with 60-75 bhp was used for the basic Nash model through 1933, but more interesting were the "Twin Ignition" models, a six and an eight. "Twin Ignition" meant that the engine had two sets of spark plugs and points, two condensers, and two coils, operating from a single distributor. The first Twin Ignition Six had appeared in 1928; the Eight was new for 1930.

Buick, which Charles Nash had once headed in his GM days, traditionally espoused overhead valves, so it was not surprising to see the same configuration on Nash Twin Ignition engines. The T.I. Six disappeared after 1930, but the Eight carried on, gaining in displacement and horsepower. The 1930 T.I. Eight had 298.6 cubic inches and 100 bhp. It reached as high as 322 cid and 125 bhp for 1932-34, but cost factors and the public's demand for more economical engines finally caused Nash to drop this big engine. T.I. Eights of 1935-39 had a much smaller 260.8-cid engine, which had first been introduced as the 1932 Special

1930 Nash Twin Ignition Eight dual-cowl phaeton

1931 Nash Ambassador touring sedan

1931 Nash Six delivery car

Nash & LaFayette

Eight. All Nash eights had nine main bearings.

The Twin Ignition cars of 1930 wore classic upright styling which continued right through 1934, despite a general industry shift toward rounded streamlined shapes. Twin Ignition Sixes rode 118- and 128.3-inch wheelbases; Eights used 124- and 133-inch wheelbases. The longer chassis carried seven-passenger sedans and limousines in both series, along with tourers, coupes, cabriolets, and Ambassadors in the Eight range. The Ambassadors, luxuriously upholstered for five well-heeled passengers, were nicely proportioned cars. No Nashes have been certified as Classics by the CCCA, but if any Nash deserves this distinction, the long-wheelbase Twin Ignition Eight of 1930-34 is the most likely candidate.

Charles Nash believed in offering a lot for the money, and his cars bristled with innovations. The Twin Ignition Eights had cowl vents, dashboard starter buttons, shatterproof glass, and automatic radiator vents in 1930; downdraft carburetors and Bijur automatic chassis lubrication in 1931; "Syncro-Safety Shift" (with gear lever sprouting from the dash) and optional free-wheeling in 1932; combination ignition and steering wheel locks in 1933; and aircraft-type instruments in 1934. Many of these features were shared with the cheaper side-valve Eight offered in 1931-33 for the 870/970 Standard series. This engine's displacement (227.2-247.4 cid) and output (78-85 bhp) were midway between the side-valve Six and Twin Ignition eight. Prices were arranged accordingly in these years: about $800-$900 for Sixes, $900-$1100 for side-valve Eights, and $1300 to as much as $2400 for T.I. Eights.

Like most companies, Nash was damaged badly by the Depression. While Kenosha regularly built over 100,000 cars a year in the late '20s, it never reached that figure in the 1930s. Throughout the decade Nash ranked 11th, 12th, or 13th in production. The bottom was reached in 1933 when output totaled less than 15,000 cars. Thus, 1934 was clearly a year for new approaches. Restyling of the big Nashes was postponed for a year, while resources were put into a revived nameplate thought to be just right for those times, the LaFayette.

While the LaFayette of 1934-36 was hardly in the class of its V-8 forebear, it was an attractively styled car with a highly competitive price: $585 to $715. It rode a 113-inch wheelbase—the shortest chassis Nash offered in the '30s—and carried the 217.8-cid six formerly used in 1930-33 Nashes. Horsepower was 75 to 83 bhp. The all-steel bodies were offered mainly in sedan form, though a LaFayette victoria was added in 1936. LaFayette volume was approximately 12,700 units in 1934, 9300 in 1935, and 14,000 in 1936. Its

1936 LaFayette three-passenger coupe

1934 LaFayette five-passenger sedan

1936 LaFayette four-door sedan

1937 Nash Ambassador Eight sedan (with Babe Ruth)

1939 Nash LaFayette four-door sedan

share of overall Kenosha production was 44 percent in 1934, but it dropped to about 25 percent in succeeding years. Since there seemed to be no sales advantage in continuing LaFayette as a separate make, the name became just a series in the Nash line from 1937 on.

Nash built its one-millionth car in 1934, and looked forward to better times. A severe cropping of the '34 model lineup resulted in only three separate series, all with overhead-valve engines: the Big Six (234.8 cid/88 bhp); the Advanced Eight (260.8 cid/100 bhp); and the Ambassador Eight (322 cid/125 bhp). In 1935, hydraulic brakes arrived for all Nash models, but the Ambassador lost its smooth 322 engine and shared the 260.8-cid unit with the Advanced Eight.

The long-awaited Nash restyle of 1935 (called Aeroform design) was a good one. The cars were now fully updated with sweeping fastback or curved notchback bodies and skirted fenders. Some sedans were available with swept-down decks and concealed spare tires. The hood was louvered, the radiator vee'd, and the wheels were all-steel "artillery" types. Nash had a good year in 1935, producing close to 45,000 cars. In 1936, it did even better, reaching 53,000 units with the help of the low-priced 400 series on a 117-inch wheelbase.

For 1937, Nash maintained its three-model lineup. The Nash LaFayette, with a 234.8-cid six and 90 bhp, replaced the 400 on the same chassis; the Ambassador Six rode a 121-inch wheelbase and used the 234.8-cid engine with 105 bhp; the Ambassador Eight, on a 125-inch wheelbase, continued to use the 260.8-cid Twin Ignition eight and had 105 bhp. This spread of engine types and wheelbases would continue throughout the end of the decade, with horsepower gradually increasing. For 1939, horsepower was 99 on the LaFayette, 105 on the Ambassador Six, and 115 on the Ambassador Eight. Styling became more conventional as the years passed. The 1937 Nash line bore a distinct resemblance to the Airstream Chryslers, for instance, and this seemed to satisfy the public: Nash had its best year of the '30s with 85,949 cars.

In 1938, however, Kenosha marched back down the hill it had climbed so laboriously. Production sank to 32,000 units and the new Nash-Kelvinator Corporation

lost $7.7 million. Styling was unattractive, though the major cause of the sales drop was the 1938 recession. The cars had received a severe facelift, and now resembled the dumpier GM products. Yet despite the unsuccessful appearance changes and a bad year for the economy in general, Nash still had an innovation that year: the "Weather-Eye" combination heating and ventilation system. This pioneering product was one of the best "climatizers" ever invented, and it remained so for the next 20 years.

A total restyle was a necessity for 1939, and fortunately, it was a good one. The ponderous '38 bodies with their busy front ends and bustle backs were eliminated. The Nash and Nash LaFayette now featured a smooth, well-integrated front end with flush-fitting headlamps. A prow-like hood blended with a center grille composed of narrow vertically stacked bars, and flanked either side by chromed catwalk grilles. The cars looked neat and trim combining all the best design elements of the art-deco era. Nash production, at 66,000 units, was more than double that of 1938. The 1939 LaFayette came in Special and Deluxe form. The Ambassador Six and Eight featured coupes and sedans, plus a five-passenger cabriolet. Prices were competitive: $800-$950 for LaFayettes, $900-$1050 for Ambassador Sixes, and $1200-$1300 for Ambassador Eights. Although Nash-Kelvinator lost $1.6 million this year, the future looked brighter in 1939 than it had for the last ten years.

Nashes of the 1930s are not expensive today. While the big, open Ambassador Eights of 1930-34 can command up to $10,000 in mint restored condition, most prices range well below half that figure. LaFayette prices are still down around the $2000-$3000 level and the cars are good buys, even though they are unpretentious in every way. The beautifully executed Ambassadors of 1939 are perhaps the sleepers of the group. In design, almost any year's Nash, except the 1938, is a good one. The appropriate organization is the Nash Car Club, c/o James Dworschack, Route 1, Clinton, Iowa 52732.

photo credits: *American Motors Corporation*

Oldsmobile & Viking

Olds Motor Works, Lansing, Michigan

There was a time when Oldsmobile, not Ford, was number one among car producers. That was in 1903-05, when Lansing rolled to success with Ransom Eli Olds' little curved dash runabout, the world's first mass-production automobile. Actually, Olds built his first experimental car in 1891, and had started production by 1897. That made Olds the second oldest car maker (after Studebaker) among all makes offered in the '30s. But age and tradition count for little in the automobile industry. Soon after Ransom Olds left to form the Reo company in 1904, a decline set in at Oldsmobile. General Motors bought the firm in 1909, but even that didn't immediately help sales. It wasn't

1930 Viking Eight roadster

1930 Viking Eight Deluxe rumble-seat roadster

1932 Oldsmobile Eight four-door sedan

until Olds produced a side-valve V-8 in 1916 that its cars really began to sell well again. Lansing's best years between 1916 and 1930 were 1921 and 1929, when it finished ninth in sales.

In the '30s though, Oldsmobile blossomed, especially under the leadership of general manager Charles L. McCuen. Oldsmobile featured sychromesh transmission from 1931, "Knee-Action" independent front suspension from 1934, semi-automatic transmission in 1937-38, and Hydra-Matic Drive from 1939. The worst Depression year for the division was 1932, when only 17,500 cars were produced. After that, Oldsmobile recovered rapidly. Lansing built 183,000 cars and finished fifth in 1935; it built even more in 1936, and still more in 1937. Though the 1938 recession cut Olds output to less than 100,000 units, the division rallied quickly by building 160,000 cars in 1939 and a record-shattering 215,000 in 1940. By the end of the '30s, Oldsmobile's future was secure.

Olds' modern role as the "experimental division" of GM really started in the '30s. General manager McCuen had served as chief engineer before becoming general manager in 1933. To take his place as chief engineer, he recruited Harold T. Youngren, a brilliant innovator. Under Youngren were experimental engineering manager Jack Wolfram and dynomometer wizard Harold Metzel. Both Wolfram and Metzel themselves became Olds general managers in later years; Youngren left in 1945 to help develop Ford's engineering department on the basis of his experience at Olds.

One unfortunate product which McCuen didn't have to deal with as general manager was Oldsmobile's junior make, Viking. This nameplate was born in 1929 and lasted just one year. Unlike the Buick Marquette or Cadillac LaSalle, the Viking was an up-market extension of its parent. The 1930 Oldsmobile was powered by an underwhelming 197.5-cid six and had a 113.5-inch wheelbase; the Viking rode a 125-inch wheelbase and used a 259.5-cid V-8. Overall, the Viking resembled the LaSalle, but its V-8 engine was unique. Unlike the long-stroke engines of the day, it had almost square dimensions: a 3.38-inch bore and 3.63-inch stroke. Its chain-driven camshaft actuated a row of horizontal valves mounted between the cylinder banks, and output was a decent 81 bhp at 3000 rpm. While the 1930 Oldsmobile Standard, Special, and Deluxe Sixes sold for about $900-$1200, the Viking cost some $1600, and offered deluxe coachwork with luxurious trim. Olds built a modest 6612 Vikings in model year 1929, and such a car was literally certain to fail in the economic climate of the Depression. Viking's 1930 model year production was only 1390 and the make was dropped for 1931 as Olds soldiered on with its short-wheelbase Six, which came in Standard and Deluxe versions that year.

1933 Oldsmobile Six four-door sedan

For 1932, the six was bored out to 213.3 cid and achieved 74 bhp. Sixes also had a longer wheelbase, 116.5 inches, which was shared with a new Oldsmobile Eight. Unlike the Viking, this new eight-cylinder engine was a conventional inline unit with side valves, though it did produce 87 bhp out of 240.3 cubic inches.

Both the six and eight were good engines—quiet, smooth and reliable. Both received major improvements as the decade wore on, such as aluminum pistons in 1936. A major redesign in 1937 saw the eight bored out to 257.1 cid for 110 bhp while the six was

bored to 229.7 cid and yielded 95 bhp. In addition, the '37 engines had full-length water jacketing, stiffer piston skirts and crankshaft, stronger cams and valve lifters, and longer valve guides. In this form, the eight continued without change until 1949, when it was honorably retired in favor of the new overhead-valve "Rocket" V-8. The six had reached a displacement of close to 260 cid when it was phased out of production in 1950.

One of the reasons Olds suffered relatively less than most companies in the '30s was that it cut its losses more quickly. The Viking was killed off as soon as its lack of success became evident and was replaced by a conventional eight-cylinder car more attuned to the public's tastes at the time. Oldsmobile also resisted constant changes to its model lineup. From 1933 to '38, it offered only two basic models, a Six and an Eight, on two wheelbases. Chassis design was not changed much, although the '34s introduced Knee-Action front suspension and the '37s received a new, lighter X-braced frame. Sixes stuck to a wheelbase of 115/117 inches; Eights had 119/124-inch spans.

Olds styling was also fairly conservative: formal and upright for 1930-32; slightly streamlined, with an angled radiator and skirted fenders for 1933; and "potato-shaped" for 1934-35. After 1935, design evolutions occurred at a steady pace. Even though Olds

1934 Oldsmobile Six sport coupe

1935 Oldsmobile Eight five-passenger coach

1936 Oldsmobile Six rumble-seat convertible coupe

Oldsmobile & Viking

used the same GM B-body as LaSalle and the smaller Buicks, its cars managed to retain an individual appearance. The 1936s and 1937s had more massive front ends with cross-hatched or horizontal bar grilles; the 1938s and 1939s had headlamp pods partly faired into the front fender aprons, and Harley Earl's "twin catwalk" auxilliary grilles on either side of the main grillework. Prices were accurately placed in a competitive market area below Buick and LaSalle and above Pontiac. The six/eight-cylinder sedan cost $825/$1100 in 1932; $755/$965 in 1934, $795/$910 in 1936, and $970/$1081 in 1938. Olds management also quickly cancelled any body styles that didn't sell: The phaeton was gone after 1930, the roadster vanished after 1931, and a convertible sedan was never even listed in the '30s. Aside from choices in wheelbase, engine, and trim, there were styling options such as dual outside spares in the early '30s, and a choice between outside spare or "trunkback" sedans in the latter part of the decade. Convertible coupes were low-production items. In 1937, for example, Oldsmobile built only 1619 six-cylinder convertibles and 630 Eights out of a model year run of about 200,000 units.

Where Oldsmobile won its reputation for innovation

1937 Oldsmobile Eight convertible coupe

1939 Oldsmobile Series 70 Club Coupe

and experimentation was in transmission design. Twice during the '30s, Olds introduced important gearbox ideas. The second of these—Hydra-Matic for 1939—later became the standard for the industry in automatic transmissions.

The first new transmission was a semi-automatic four-speed unit introduced on the L-37 eight-cylinder cars in May, 1937. Called "Automatic Safety Transmission," it operated like—but was not mechanically identical to—Chrysler's subsequent Fluid Drive. At rest, the driver depressed a conventional clutch pedal and moved the gear lever to a Low or High range. In motion, the car shifted up or down between first and second in "Low," and first, third, and fourth in "High." It operated through two planetary units, each with one brake and one clutch band. Shifts were made automatically via oil pressure. The shift points were preset according to vehicle speed.

Oldsmobile claimed up to 15 percent better gas mileage with the semi-automatic, mainly due to a higher-than-standard rear axle ratio on cars so equipped. The "safety" part of the name referred to the fact that it required relatively little gear shifting and ostensibly allowed the driver to keep his hands on the wheel. The option was offered on all models in 1938, and some 28,000 were installed altogether. The semi-automatic's real claim to fame, however, is that it led to Hydra-Matic in 1939.

Hydra-Matic also had four speeds, but was a completely automatic transmission using a fluid coupling and a complicated system of clutches and brake bands. It cost only $57 extra on any Oldsmobile (semi-automatic had cost $80), but its price was probably not indicative of its true manufacturing cost. High-volume sales would largely make up for developmental expenses, and they did. By the late '40s and early '50s, Hydra-Matic was being used by Cadillac and Pontiac as well as Oldsmobile—not to mention several independents (Nash, Hudson, Frazer, Kaiser) who offered it on their own cars. Introduced along with the new transmission for 1939 was a three-model Olds line. In addition to the Six (now Series 60) and Eight (Series 80) there was a middle-range Series 70. This used the 80's 120-inch wheelbase and the six-cylinder engine tuned to deliver a few extra horsepower. A few years later the 80 eight-cylinder series would become the famous "88."

Oldsmobiles of all years in the 1930s are still relatively cheap on the collector market today. The pre-1934 models offer classic-era styling, while the post-1934s have a great deal of technical interest. Vikings, though they offered no important innovations, are certainly collector's items due to their extreme scarcity. No Oldsmobiles are rated as Classics, but the marque has a 2000-member following in the Oldsmobile Club of America, Box 1498 SMS, Fairfield, Connecticut 06430.

photo credits: *Oldsmobile Division, General Motors Corporation*

Packard

Packard Motor Car Company
Detroit, Michigan

For the past several years, some classic-car enthusiasts have engaged in "debunking" the Packard legend. Numerous articles and many graphs, charts, and tables have been created to demonstrate that Packard was *not* the preeminent luxury car of the Classic Era (the period beginning roughly in 1925 and ending with World War II). But the revisionists have all missed a salient point: Through 1935 at least, Packard was the unquestioned luxury car in the *minds* of wealthy buyers. To the "old money," a Duesenberg was a vulgar extravagance, and a Cadillac was for the *nouveau riche*—sixteen cylinders or otherwise. The Duesenberg's superior performance and the Cadillac's superior refinement were less important to these people than the image such cars are supposed to have. To them, Packard was "the supreme combination of all that is fine in motorcars." Technologically, it may not have been the "Standard of the World." But sociologically, it was the Standard of America—even for people who couldn't afford one. In 1929, Packard's was the second most widely held stock next to that of General Motors—and there were more Packard stockholders than Packard owners.

Packard's great fame had probably begun with its 48-bhp Six in 1912. Then in 1915, Packard leapfrogged Cadillac's new V-8 with a V-12, the fabled Twin Six model. Shortly after the Twin Six was dropped in 1923, a new straight eight arrived. Packard did produce a less prestigious six beginning in 1921, but that model disappeared during the '20s and eight-cylinder engines maintained the Packard reputation from then on.

For a builder devoted singlemindedly to luxury cars, Packard had a remarkable production record. From 1925, it had regularly outproduced Cadillac, even after its GM rival introduced the LaSalle in 1927. With the exceptions of 1931, 1932, and 1934, Packard volume continued to exceed Cadillac/LaSalle output, right through until World War II. But Packard's post-1934 production rested on models other than all-out luxury cars. The 1935 One-Twenty saved the company from the Depression and helped raise production to record levels.

The 1930 Packard line was continued from 1929 comprised entirely of straight eights. There were two engines: a 320-cid unit with 90 bhp, and a 385-cid engine with 106-145 bhp. The 320 remained in production throughout the decade unchanged except for horsepower—it had reached 130 bhp by 1936. The 385-cid "Super Eight" powerplant continued through 1936, by which time it was developing 150 bhp. Packard wheelbases in 1930 ranged from 127.5 to 140.5 inches. Officially, Packard did not observe model years in this period; its cars were known by a "series" number which dated from 1923. Historians have since applied model year designations to each series for ease of recognition, and 1930 coincides with the Seventh Series.

Packard styling, like that of Mercedes today, was purposely conservative, and followed a consistent theme from year to year. One of the big arguments the company used on potential customers was that a Packard didn't depreciate like lesser cars. Since it was common in those days for customers to replace an outmoded body with a new one while retaining the same chassis, the company argued that a more expensive Packard was actually cheaper to own in the long run than a middle-priced car. Packard styling hallmarks—the ox-yoke radiator and hood shape, the red hexagon hub emblem, the pelican crest of James Ward Packard—were prominently displayed on each successive model. Body styling was by a brilliant German named Werner Gubitz. Although custom body builders contributed their own ideas to Packard styling, the area from the cowl forward was never altered much. Seventh Series cars followed this tradition, with a massive front end, twin-bar bumpers, and beautifully curved, unskirted fenders. A minor recognition point was the top of their headlight and parking light rims, which duplicated the shape of the grille.

The Standard Eight offered the least pretentious Packard bodies on a relatively short wheelbase: sedans, phaetons, roadsters, tourings, coupes, convertibles, and limousines. These ranged in price from $2375 to $2775 and accounted for about 75 percent of Packard production. Next came the dashing Speedster Eight, powered by a 145-bhp version of the 385 engine. It used a 134-inch wheelbase for its lithe-looking boattail and standard roadster, phaeton, victoria, and sedan. Speedsters cost the world in 1930: $5200 to $6000. Only 150 were built, and the model disappeared in 1931. A 106-bhp 385 engine powered the long-wheelbase Custom and Deluxe Eights. Although these cars were generally seen with closed bodies, they were also available with phaeton, roadster, and convertible bodies designed by Packard and various custom coachbuilders. They ranged in price from $3190 to $5140. You can get a better idea of the real cost of a Packard by considering that $5000 would buy a rather nice house in 1930, and is equivalent to about $35,000 today.

The 1931 Eighth Series offered Packard's two engines in three model lines, the Standard, Custom, and Deluxe Eights. The Standard now included a range of "Individual Custom" models on a 134.5-inch wheelbase and comprised a convertible sedan and victoria by Dietrich, plus Packard's own cabriolets, landaulets, and town cars. Horsepower rose to 100 bhp on Standard Eights and 120 bhp for the Custom and Deluxe. Mechanically, the Eighth Series gained an automatic

Packard

Bijur chassis lubrication system and power output was increased via modified intake and exhaust passages similar to those seen on the 1930 Speedster Eight. Packard also designed a quick-shift mechanism for its four-speed gearbox to reduce gearchanging effort. In 1932, however, the company switched to a three-speed all-synchromesh transmission.

Styling in 1932 was similar to 1930-31, except that bodies were lower for a more streamlined appearance. Two significant Ninth Series models were the Twin Six and Light Eight. The former bore no relationship to Packard's Twin Six of 1916-23. It had actually been designed for a front-wheel-drive layout which had been shelved before the car reached production. The engine had four main bearings, a capacity of 445.5 cid, and produced 160 bhp at 3200 rpm. In 1935, it was stroked to 475 cid and 175 bhp, in which form it remained through the last of the Twelves in 1939. ("Twelve" replaced the "Twin Six" name in 1933.)

Though a fairly low numerical axle ratio was theoretically available, most Twelves had numerical ratios of 4.41:1 or higher. They were designed for smooth, relatively shift-free motoring rather than high performance. Packard claimed that a sustained 100 mph was well within the capabilities of the V-12 engine, but that was under test conditions. Off the floor, Twelves usually ran out of breath at about 90 mph. At 60 or 70 mph, however, they were whisper quiet and highly refined.

Twin Sixes and Twelves of the 1932-34 period shared the bodies and 142.5/147.5-inch wheelbases with the Super Eight series. Despite their prestigious reputation and advertising which billed them as the ultimate Packards, factory-bodied Twelves were originally only $100-$200 more expensive than the Super Eights. The price gap grew wider as time went on, however, and custom-bodied Twelves soon cost considerably more than Super Eights: The 1932 Dietrich sport phaeton body listed for $6500 on the V-12 chassis, compared to $5800 on the Super Eight platform. In 1935, when "senior model" production was consolidated to make space for the high-volume One-Twenty, the Twelve shifted to 139- and 144-inch wheelbases; contemporary Super Eights also offered these sizes, and a slightly smaller wheelbase, too, with the same general range of body styles. Custom body offerings decreased as coachbuilders went out of business or were bought out by other companies. In 1938, for ex-

1932 Packard Deluxe Eight convertible victoria by Dietrich

1932 Packard Deluxe Eight coupe by Dietrich

1933 Packard Light Eight sedan

1933 Packard Twelve all-weather town car by LeBaron

ample, custom Twelves and Super Eights listed by Packard numbered only four: the Rollston all-weather cabriolet and town car, and the Brunn touring and all-weather cabriolet. These ranged in price from $5790 to $7475 as Super Eights, and from $6730 to $8510 as Twelves.

It is important to note that production of the most luxurious Packards was only a tiny percentage of the factory's total output, especially after 1934. In 1932, Packard built just 549 Twin Sixes. High figures for the V-12 chassis were 960 units in the Eleventh Series (1934) and 1300 in the Fifteenth Series (1937). Super Eight production was greater, reaching a record of 5793 units in 1937 and totaling 3920 in 1939. But these were not sufficient quantities to keep a small independent alive in the Depression. What kept Packard going were its volume cars: first, the 1932 Light Eight and later, the more successful One-Twenty (eight) and One-Ten (six).

Packard didn't have the luxury of financial support from a mighty parent corporation like GM or Ford. Therefore, the company had to introduce new products more suitable for the Depression-era market earlier than Cadillac or Lincoln. As a result, the Light Eight—Packard's first car in the medium-price field—arrived two years before Cadillac's smaller, cheaper LaSalle and four years before Lincoln's Zephyr. It used the Standard Eight's 320-cid engine, rated for 1932 at 110 bhp, and had its own 127.6-inch-wheelbase chassis. Four models—coupe-sedan, coupe-roadster, coupe, and sedan—sold for $1750-$1795. This amounted to a price difference equal to the cost of a Ford V-8 compared with the next lowest-priced model, the Standard Eight.

The Light Eight was a quality product, built with the same meticulous care as other Packards. It was faster than the Standard Eight, owing to its lighter chassis, but it was chunky looking, owing to its shorter wheelbase. Unfortunately, their low prices made the 6750 Light Eights sold that year more of a disadvantage than a benefit. The cars cost almost as much to make as the Standard Eights, yet they sold for $500-$850 less, so

the factory was lucky to break even on any Light Eight it sold. In 1933, the range was dropped. Packard president Alvan Macauley then began searching the ranks of GM executives for someone wise in the ways of high-volume production to help the firm develop a profitable middle-priced car.

Packard lost $7 million in 1932, much of it on the Light Eight, but the company realized a $500,000 profit in 1933, and its proportion of sales in the high-priced field was 38 percent—well above Cadillac's market share. The trouble was that there was hardly a high-priced market left. Macauley's recruiting campaign was vigorous. He ended up with Max Gilman, "that hardboiled guy in New York," who had started out as a Brooklyn truck salesman in 1919; and George T. Christopher, a production expert whom Macauley enticed out of retirement from General Motors. Gilman astutely built the image of a forthcoming new Packard, wheting the public's appetite. Christopher overhauled most of the factory for high-volume production, modernizing it from end to end. The fruit of their efforts was announced on January 6, 1935—the Packard One-Twenty.

The One-Twenty was a dramatic departure from Packard tradition. Its price, from $980 to $1095, was almost half that of the unmourned Light Eight. It was

1934 Packard Super Eight all-weather cabriolet by LeBaron

Packard

aimed precisely at those people who had always wanted a Packard but could never before afford one. As such, it retained traditional Packard hallmarks, like the ox-yoke radiator/hood styling, red hexagon wheel hub emblems, and conservative body lines. Seven models were offered on a 120-inch wheelbase (hence the car's name). The engine, designed largely by former GM people, was a straightforward L-head eight with 257.2 cubic inches and 110 bhp. It had five main bearings; a 2.75-inch crankshaft; counterweighted; overlapping journals; a heavily ribbed engine block, ample water jacketing; and individual exhaust ports for each cylinder. It was easy on gas, smooth in performance, and granite strong. The 1936 and later One-Twenty models had a stroke increase, which yielded 282 cid and 120 bhp. Typical performance for these cars was 85 mph top speed and 0-60 mph in less than 20 seconds—pretty decent for any 3500-pound car in the prewar years.

In 1936, a convertible sedan bearing "Dietrich" body plates was added to the One-Twenty line. (Actually Ray Dietrich personally had nothing to do with its de-sign but his name had been owned by Murray since the early '30s.) In 1937, a wagon, three Deluxe closed models, and a long-wheelbase sedan and limousine appeared. Packard sold One-Twenties like nickel hamburgers. For calendar year 1935, the company soared to ninth place in production with over 52,000 units. Output hit about 81,000 in 1936, and 110,000 in 1937. The 1938 recession slowed volume to about 50,000, but in 1939, production picked up again to about 77,000 units and remained strong through World War II.

The production record of 1937 was also due to the success of another even less expensive Packard, the One-Ten, known in 1938-39 as the Packard Six. This model had a One-Twenty-derived engine which displaced 236.5 cubic inches for 100 bhp. The One-Ten rode a 115-inch wheelbase in 1937. Displacement was up to 245 cid and wheelbase to 122 inches for 1938-39, although horsepower remained unchanged. The line-up was similar to the One-Twenty, but prices were some $150 cheaper model for model, and the One-Ten outsold the One-Twenty by a ratio of 13 to 10 in 1937. Its six was not as smooth or powerful as the eight-cylinder One-Twenty engine, but it did offer excellent gas mileage and adequate performance.

With the Fifteenth Series 1937 One-Ten, Packard completed its transformation from a builder of exclu-

1934 Packard Twelve convertible coupe by Dietrich

1936 Packard One-Twenty sedan

1937 Packard One-Twenty station wagon (prototype)

1937 Packard Eight club sedan

1937 Packard Twelve sedan

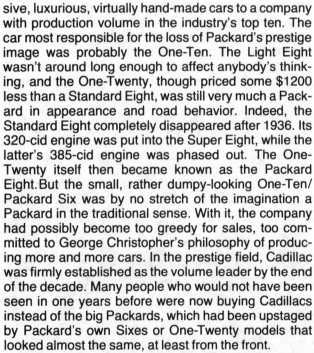

1939 Packard Eight Safari wagon

1939 Packard Twelve all-weather cabriolet by Rollston

sive, luxurious, virtually hand-made cars to a company with production volume in the industry's top ten. The car most responsible for the loss of Packard's prestige image was probably the One-Ten. The Light Eight wasn't around long enough to affect anybody's thinking, and the One-Twenty, though priced some $1200 less than a Standard Eight, was still very much a Packard in appearance and road behavior. Indeed, the Standard Eight completely disappeared after 1936. Its 320-cid engine was put into the Super Eight, while the latter's 385-cid engine was phased out. The One-Twenty itself then became known as the Packard Eight. But the small, rather dumpy-looking One-Ten/ Packard Six was by no stretch of the imagination a Packard in the traditional sense. With it, the company had possibly become too greedy for sales, too committed to George Christopher's philosophy of producing more and more cars. In the prestige field, Cadillac was firmly established as the volume leader by the end of the decade. Many people who would not have been seen in one years before were now buying Cadillacs instead of the big Packards, which had been upstaged by Packard's own Sixes or One-Twenty models that looked almost the same, at least from the front.

Another factor in Packard's loss of prestige in the high-dollar market was the decline of its inimitable styling. Surely the Packards of 1933-35, with their skirted fenders, vee'd radiators, and upright lines, were among the most beautiful cars of the decade. The 1934 Dietrich convertible victoria, on either the Super Eight or Twelve chassis, is thought by many to be the definitive classic car. But 1935 ushered in the One-

Twenty, which from the cowl back was little more distinctive than a middle-priced Oldsmobile. The Packard hood and radiator were simply not enough to maintain the style—and the quality image—which had been such a big part of the firm's reputation in earlier years. Packard continued to build some lovely cars in the late '30s: The Darrin victorias which appeared in 1938 are among the prettiest of the era, but these specials were relatively scarce.

Prewar Packards generally have only one price these days: high. Figures of $50,000 and even $75,000 are not unknown for prime-condition open models, particularly Twelves and Super Eights. Closed models with Classic status sell for much less, though. If you don't mind taking on a restoration job, you can still find them for $4000-$6000. (CCCA-recognized Classics include all 1930-34 models, all 1935-38s except One-Twenty and One-Ten, 1939 long-wheelbase Super Eights, all 1939 Twelves, and all One-Twenty Darrin victorias.) Standard One-Twenty and One-Ten Six models are considerably cheaper, but even those are now becoming scarce, and prices for sporty open models are on the rise.

There are two main national Packard clubs which accept models of all periods: The Packard Club Inc., Box 2808, Oakland, California 94618, and Packards International, c/o Custom Auto Service, 302 North French Street, Santa Ana, California 92701.

photo credits: *Packard Automobile Classics; Eastern Packard Club; National Automotive History Collection, Detroit Public Library*

Pierce-Arrow

**Pierce-Arrow Motor Car Company
Buffalo, New York**

Pierce-Arrow lived in the golden age of American motoring greats—Cadillac, Duesenberg, La-Salle, Lincoln, Marmon, Packard, Peerless, Stutz, the Springfield Rolls-Royce. Peerless, like the American Rolls, was only a shadow of its former self by 1930, and of little importance as a competitor. So were Duesenberg, Marmon, and Stutz. Cadillac and Lincoln were bankrolled by big corporations and therefore had the best chance of survival among the prestige makes in the financially perilous years to come. Pierce's closest rival in the '30s was Packard; these two were the last of the great independents.

Though each make had its own distinctive appearance, they were remarkably similar in engineering. Pierce's Eight arrived in 1929, five years after Packard's, but it was technically superior and offered more performance. Pierce and Packard Twelves were evenly matched. Packard, of course, was the stronger corporation; this stemmed from the inherent advantages of its Detroit location and a more forward-looking management team. By the time Pierce updated its cars from big sixes to straight-eight engines in 1929, Packard's lead was too great to be overcome, although Pierces of the early '30s showed the marque still had potential for greatness. In engineering, styling, quality, refinement, and prestige, Pierce-Arrow and Packard marked the summit of American classic-car achievement. They acknowledged few rivals; they had no superiors.

In 1928, Pierce-Arrow was bought by Studebaker, under its accountant-turned-president, Albert R. Erskine. Pierce had been ailing for several years and was looking for a guardian angel; Erskine wanted to acquire a prestige nameplate for the burgeoning Studebaker empire. Though Erskine became its president, Pierce-Arrow continued as an independent entity under its own general manager, Arthur J. Chanter. Its own engineers, not Studebaker's, designed the 1929 Pierce-Arrow Eight.

There were two lines of Pierces, both powered by the same 366-cid, nine-bearing, 125-bhp engine. Distinctively Pierce-Arrow in design, they were enthusiastically received—and deserved to be. They were better looking, better handling, faster, lower slung, and lower priced than their six-cylinder predecessors. Pierce-Arrow sales in 1929 were over double those of 1928. Even the October, 1929 stock market crash didn't immediately affect the sales situation; volume rose through the spring of 1930. By the second quarter, sales were dropping behind 1929's level. There was no immediate concern in Buffalo, for 1930 would be Pierce's second-best year ever; 6919 units were built. The market, which had been grim before the Studebaker takeover, was again viewed with Pierce's old combination of arrogance and naiveté. The firm couldn't see the darker days ahead.

Despite the Depression and Pierce's eventual eclipse, the firm built some spectacular cars during the

1933 Pierce-Arrow Silver Arrow show car

1934 Pierce-Arrow Twelve sedan

1934 Pierce-Arrow convertible sedan by Rollston

decade. A 1930 town car created by Brunn for the Shah of Persia was typical. Originally white, it was later changed to dark blue, and had gold-plated metalwork, wolfhound fur rugs, and embroidered champagne-colored silk upholstery. Another notable Pierce was the sport phaeton built for the Silver Jubilee of Kansas City's Motor Car Dealers Association. Painted silver and upholstered in a "special blue leather," this car had hubcaps, dash, and gearshift studded with $100,000 worth of precious stones ("diamonds predominating").

Cadillac's V-16 of 1930 sent Pierce chief engineer Karl M. Wise to work on a Pierce-Arrow V-12, which was introduced for 1932. Initially, it came in two engine sizes: 398 cid with 140 bhp, and 429 cid with 150 bhp. The 398 version was soon dropped because it did not perform any better than Pierce's 385-cid eights. To keep up in the horsepower race, the Twelve was increased in capacity to 462 cubic inches for an output of 175 horsepower in 1933. Pierce-Arrow test driver Ab Jenkins took a 462 to the Bonneville Salt Flats in September, 1932. With this basically standard car, which had already seen 33,000 test miles, Jenkins piled up 2710 miles at 112.91 mph average over 24 hours. The fenders, windshield, and road equipment were then reinstalled on the car, which was immediately driven 2000 miles back across the continent to Buffalo. This run was followed by two more in 1933 and 1934, at 117.77 and 127 mph, respectively.

But multi-cylinder engines, as Marmon, Cadillac, Packard, and others were learning, were not the key to survival in the luxury-car field of the early '30s. In 1932, Pierce-Arrow lost $3 million on sales of $8 million. Reflecting the optimism shared by its Studebaker owner, Pierce had underestimated the severity of the Depression. Extensive advertising had not helped profits, nor did raising 1932 prices about $500 per car. For the first half of the year, 1523 Pierce-Arrows were sold, compared to 2987 in 1931. A total of 2241 were sold for the year, mostly to dealers and at retail through company sales outlets. Sales for the first six months of 1933 declined again, to 1020, but the company adapted to reduced demand and was able to cut operating costs.

Roy Faulkner, the dynamic former president of Auburn, took over as Pierce-Arrow sales manager in late 1932. His presence lent credence to rumors of an impending merger with Auburn, but a month after Pierce-Arrow went bankrupt in 1934, Faulkner returned to Indiana. Faulkner's promotional efforts, the Silver Arrow show cars, and Jenkins' speed records were successful—at first. The fabulous Silver Arrow of 1933 was an aesthetic success for those dark times. Radical and streamlined, it "gives you in 1933 the car of 1940," according to Pierce literature. It was a truly advanced design, although it did not inspire future Pierce-Arrow styling. Sales of Twelves were up by 200 percent in January, 1933, by 130 percent in February, and were 55 percent better than 1932 through October. But tool-and-die-makers strikes interfered with the 1933 recovery, and 300-400 late-year sales were lost.

Studebaker bankrolled Pierce losses in mid 1933, protecting the company from the effects of the Depression. But Studebaker itself was overextended, and went bankrupt in the spring of 1933. Albert Erskine committed suicide the following July. In August, Pierce-Arrow was bought by a group of businessmen and bankers. Again, the company was an independent and, ironically, now more financially healthy than Studebaker. Pierce's debts were cancelled and sales improved. The company hoped to break even at 3000 annual sales and make a million dollars profit at 4000 units. But by the end of 1933, sales had reached only 2152—500 less than the 1932 total.

The new owners appointed former general manager Arthur J. Chanter, now 43, to succeed Erskine. Chanter and Faulkner planned to expand sales and began promoting the cars with inexpensive, although elegant, black-and-white advertisements. The 1934 models were restyled, gaining a more streamlined look; the same basic style continued in 1935. Externally, the main recognition feature of a 1935 Pierce was its rearranged hood louvers (from two groups of two in 1934 to a single line of three). Internally, there was a complete rearrangement of the dashboard. Instruments were grouped in two large dials flanking the steering column: One dial incorporated oil pressure, water temperature, ammeter, and fuel level gauges; the

1935 Pierce-Arrow Twelve coupe

Pierce-Arrow

other housed a speedometer and odometer. Controls were in the center and a glovebox was on the right. An electric clock was mounted on the glovebox door.

Initial 1934 registrations were disappointing: 341 cars in the first two months versus 363 in 1933. The sales effort showed results in April-June registrations, which increased 10 percent, but losses were $681,000 for the first six months of the year, and another $176,000 was lost in July. In August, Pierce-Arrow filed for bankruptcy. Merger discussions with Auburn and Reo proved futile. Chanter sought funds from the Buffalo community and from New York banks and raised about $1 million. Reorganization followed: Pierce had to sell its retail sales branches. Factory employment, which had totaled 2200-2400 since 1930, was reduced to 600-800 workers. The reorganized company was named the Pierce-Arrow Motor Corporation, and began operations in May, 1935.

Its fiscal problems did not stop Pierce from filling newsworthy orders, such as the one detailed by *Time* in 1935: " . . . two swank blue limousines were sent to Washington. Both were rated to do 110 mph, both fitted throughout with bullet-proof glass, both had bodies armored with an invisible protection of bulletproof steel plate. One was addressed to J. Edgar Hoover . . . the other to Franklin D. Roosevelt."

In 1936, the whole line was redesigned to keep in step with current ideas of style and streamlining. Body lines were fashionably rounded. A built-in trunk with top-hinged lid incorporated a mercury switch interior

light. The rear windows were one-piece full-pivoting types instead of half-fixed as previously. Mechanical changes included an additional cruciform frame member and moving the engine farther forward. The steering box was mounted ahead of the front axle with a trailing drag link, and the radiator was moved forward several inches. Pierces had always been easy to drive, but the revised steering geometry, suspension, and weight distribution made the ride and handling of the 1936 models outstanding. Twelves now packed 185 bhp and the new Warner overdrive. Even a massive limousine could whisper along at 100 mph—uniformed chauffeur up front; tycoon, cigar, and *Wall Street Journal* in the rear. (Some cars had speedometers back there so the owner could keep an eye on the driver's lead-foot tendencies.) The 1936 continued with only minor changes through the last models of 1938.

1936 Pierce-Arrow Eight club berline

1936 Pierce-Arrow Eight Metropolitan town brougham by Brunn

Briefly during 1936, it looked as if Pierce-Arrow had turned the corner. Registrations showed a 25 percent gain for the first third of the year. But sales soon tapered off to below the 1935 level, and car production ceased in 1937, except for manufacture of auto show models and spare parts. The 1938 Pierce-Arrows were introduced in October, 1937, but only 30 cars were registered by the end of the following year.

The success of Packard and Lincoln with their medium-priced lines inspired schemes for another reorganization of Pierce in 1937. In August, the company announced plans to raise $10.7 million through sale of its stock to produce 25,000 medium-priced cars, plus 4800 trailers and 1200 luxury Pierce-Arrows. The company proposed to turn over management duties to Postmaster General James A. Farley, then intending to leave the Roosevelt Administration. But none of this came to pass. Farley had received similar offers from Studebaker and Willys, which he rejected, too, because they all required him to use his influence with the government, presumably to obtain contract work or federal loans. A second Pierce bankruptcy was declared in December, 1937. For the first 17 months from July, 1936, through November, 1937, losses had been nearly $250,000. Liquidation of the company's assets was ordered in 1938.

Why did Pierce-Arrow wait so long before considering a medium-priced car? There are several reasons. Through 1932, the firm's share of the total market was constant, and its share of the prestige market actually increased. During 1933, summer and fall sales increases, together with a higher percentage of V-12 sales and the general industry recovery, all indicated that the three-year sales decline had been reversed.

The Model 836A was actually an attempt at a lower-priced car introduced in March, 1934. It sold for only $2195, low for a Pierce-Arrow. But this was not sufficiently less than prices for the standard models, which began at $2795. The 1935 reorganization would have been jeopardized if the company admitted that production could only continue with a cheaper car, given the tooling costs for any sort of new product in those days. Pierce publicity unwittingly gave a clue to its insoluble problems when it boasted: "Pierce-Arrow's floor area, if used for ordinary mass production, would have a capacity four times that possible under Pierce-Arrow methods."

Pierces of the '30s were superb road machines. Their engines were powerful, smooth, and quiet, offering outstanding acceleration and hill-climbing ability. Braking, steering, and handling were all of a high order, yet tuning and maintenance were straightforward. Though Pierce-Arrow lacked the enormous technical resources of GM, its cars remained comparable with Cadillac's through the decade. Success, however, has always been on the side of the big battalions. Thus, America's pioneer grand marque—built by highly skilled craftsmen in a plant run by old New England gentlemen, the carriage of magnates and maharajahs—passed into history.

The marque is remembered today by the well-established Pierce-Arrow Society, and its club publication entitled *The Arrow*. The Society's address is 135 Edgerton Street, Rochester, New York 14607.

photo credits: *Applegate & Applegate Collection, Maurice D. Hendry*

Plymouth

Plymouth Division, Chrysler Corporation
Detroit, Michigan

The name for Chrysler's low-priced car was suggested by sales manager Joseph W. Frazer after Plymouth Rock, Massachusetts. Walter Chrysler wasn't sure if people would recognize the connotation, so Frazer reminded him of a well-known farm product. "Every farmer in America's heard of Plymouth Binder Twine," ex-farmboy Chrysler replied—and Plymouth it was. The car was a success from the day it debuted in 1928. At first, Plymouths were available only from

1931 Plymouth PA two-passenger coupe

1931 Plymouth PA convertible coupe

1932 Plymouth PB convertible sedan

Chrysler dealers, but by 1930, demand was high enough for the company to give franchises to Dodge and DeSoto dealers, too. This was excellent strategy. It insulated dealers of the higher-priced cars from the Depression, and it vastly increased the number of Plymouth outlets.

The 1930 Plymouth shared many styling features with other Chrysler makes. Its engine was increased in size from 1929 and was an L-head four with 196 cid and 48 bhp. Prices of the "New Finer Plymouth" were $590-$695—more than Ford and Chevrolet, although Chrysler insisted buyers got more for their money. In an age of wood-framed bodies, for example, Plymouth followed Chrysler practice in using all-steel construction. Plymouth also had four-wheel hydraulic brakes, while Ford and Chevrolet used mechanical brakes for several more years. The Depression was definitely on by 1930, but because of its 68,000 unit sales and a record eighth place finish, Walter Chrysler was satisfied with Plymouth's sales performance. In future years he'd be even happier.

The first new Plymouth since the nameplate premiered came in 1931, the product of approximately $2.5 million worth of development. Though the four-cylinder engine was retained, its front and rear mounts were lined with heavy rubber to insulate the powerplant from the frame. The result, as Plymouth put it, was new "Floating Power." The engine was able to "float" from side to side on its rubber mounts, which kept vibration to a minimum. This was a relatively small innovation, but in a low-priced car its effect was astonishing. Plymouth advertising made the most of it by claiming that its new model PA had "the smoothness of an eight and the economy of a four." A common sales ploy often used by dealers was to blindfold prospective customers and take them for a ride in the four-cylinder Plymouth. Then, they'd drive them around in rival four-cylinder cars, and finally ask prospects to guess which car they thought had eight cylinders. No guesses allowed as to which one they always chose. . . .

The 1931 PA model offered seven body styles, all on a 109-inch wheelbase. It had free-wheeling as well as "Floating Power" and its other 1930 features. Most important, Plymouth finished third in production that year, the first time ever the make had scored that well. And Plymouth would remain in third place for the next 23 years.

Plymouth was one of the very few cars that actually increased production between 1930 and 1931. It even gained in 1932 and 1933, two of the roughest Depression years for the industry as a whole. Plymouth output reached a record 527,177 units in 1936, but finally dropped a little in 1937. The 1938 recession saw Plymouth build only about 300,000 cars, but in 1939 it rallied, and by 1940 it was over the half-million mark

1933 Plymouth PC four-door sedan

again. There was good reason for all this: Plymouths were good-looking, well built, soundly engineered automobiles, and they offered outstanding value.

The new 1932 Plymouths were introduced in February of that year. While still a four-cylinder type, the engine now had 65 bhp, which was more than many larger powerplants offered. For the first time, a convertible sedan was offered—Chrysler evidently felt comfortable enough now to dabble with less popular body styles. Advertising asked the public to "Look at All Three," to compare Plymouth with its Ford and Chevy rivals. Against that competition, Plymouth gained considerably in market share. It was destined to do even better in 1933: A six-cylinder model was on the way.

The 1933 Plymouth six cost $9 million to develop, but was worth it in added sales. The engine displaced only 189.6 cubic inches, but produced 70 bhp—more horses for fewer cubic inches than the 1932 four. The six was enlarged to 201.3 cid in 1934, and remained that size for the rest of the decade. From 1936, it produced 82 bhp—more than adequate for a car with a base price of only $495 in standard coupe form. Plymouth performance was also improved by virtue of the new car's lightness compared to previous models. The '33 rode a two-inch shorter wheelbase than its predecessor and the six-cylinder sedan weighed about 300 pounds less than its 1932 four-cylinder counterpart. With the new engine came the traditional winged-lady hood mascot and chrome-plated radiator shell. The shell was later painted to match the body color.

A favorite publicity stunt of the time was to roll a new Plymouth off a cliff. Down it would tumble, end over end. At the bottom, the car would be turned upright, its all-steel body little the worse for wear. Almost all Chry-

sler models were shown in such ads, but in the low-priced field, the strength of the all-steel Plymouth was an eye-opener.

The 1934 models had more streamlined styling. Fenders were skirted and the separate trunk was absorbed into the rear of the body. The millionth Plymouth rolled off the line on August 10, 1934, and Walter Chrysler raised a glass to a heck of a good idea. Independent coil-spring front suspension was first used on the '34s, of which there were two models, the PF and PG, with prices ranging between $495 and $695. The Deluxe models had safety glass and artillery-type steel wheels. The latter had found favor over wire wheels, which were starting to look distinctly out of date with the more streamlined bodies of the middle '30s. The winged-lady hood ornament was replaced by the image of the good ship Mayflower, reminding

1934 Plymouth PF four-door sedan

Plymouth

buyers of the Plymouth Rock connection.

Plymouths were completely restyled for 1935. High seat backs were introduced for the first time. Mechanically, the engines had full-length water jackets; the chassis had a stabilizer bar and better weight distribution. The '36 model had only minor styling changes, but the whole body now rested on rubber insulators, just as the engine did back in 1932. It was another first for a low-priced automobile. Plymouth's price range was now $580 to $895. The cars featured a large airplane-inspired speedometer dial in the center of the dash, and a vee'd radiator which was slightly curved at the top.

Plymouth was again restyled for 1937, this time with some consideration for safety, which was of growing interest to buyers and the industry by the late '30s. Safety glass was now standard equipment on all Chrysler Corporation cars, though the right-hand windshield wiper was still an optional accessory. All interior knobs and controls were recessed. The bottom of the dash was rounded, the top of the front seat was padded. This was the last year for the crank-operated windshield and the first year for a concealed heater blower and defroster vents. It was also the first year when a Plymouth sold for more than $1000. The top-of-the-line was the Deluxe seven-passenger sedan and limousine priced at $1095.

Plymouth entered its tenth year as a make in 1938 with a number of firsts. Its model range included the first station wagon (or "Suburban" as it was called) listed as a regular catalog model. Plymouth wagons had been available as early as 1934, but only to special order. Except for the long wheelbase seven-passen-

1935 Plymouth PJ four-door sedan

1936 Plymouth PI business coupe

ger sedans, the wagon was the most expensive model in the line at $880. Its body was all wood from the windshield back, and a lot of care was needed to keep it in sound condition: An annual sanding and varnishing was mandatory. Glass windows all around were optional, although all Suburbans came with glass in the front doors. No rear bumper was available, but the tailgate-mounted spare tire made a successful substi-

1935 Plymouth PJ convertible coupe

1937 Plymouth Deluxe coupe

1939 Plymouth Deluxe convertible sedan

hood ornament. The handbrake was moved from the middle of the floor to a position under the center of the dashboard. It's hard to say much that's positive about Plymouth's lumpy styling in 1937-38.

Ex-coachbuilder Raymond H. Dietrich fully restyled the 1939 Plymouth. The most noticeable feature of the new design was a strongly peaked prow-type front end, influenced by the Lincoln Zephyr. The cars also had a vee'd two-piece windshield instead of the single pane of glass as in past years. The headlights, now rectangular, were mounted in the front fenders; and the gearshift lever was moved from the floor to the steering column. For the first time, the canvas convertible top could be power operated, a definite selling point for the low-priced Plymouth. The last convertible sedan (revived this year for a 12-month stand) and the last rumble-seat convertible were run off in 1939, also. Three different wheelbases were offered: The Roadking and Deluxe with 114 inches, the seven-passenger models with 134 inches, and the convertible sedan's 117 inches. The '39s were the best looking Plymouths in five years—a breath of fresh styling air from their makers. They were unmistakable on the outside, and unique from behind the wheel as well: The "safety speedometer" glowed green up to 30 mph, amber from 30 to 50 mph, and red at speeds over 50 mph. Ralph Nader would have loved it.

The attractive, well engineered, fun-to-drive Plymouths of the 1930s have a growing enthusiast following today, but relatively less collector interest compared to Ford and Chevrolet. This makes Plymouth prices somewhat lower on the hobbyist market. The main organization for owners is the Plymouth 4 & 6 Cylinder Owners Club, 203 Main Street East, Cavalier, North Dakota 58220.

photo credits: *Chrysler Historical Collection*

tute. Bodies were built by the U.S. Body & Forge Company of New York and Indiana.

A new model for '38 was the Roadking at $645-$746; lower-priced Plymouths were available in sedan, open, and coupe styles. The latter lacked much of the bright decoration and creature comforts of the Deluxe series. Exterior styling was mostly a carryover from 1937, with a slight restyle for the grille, headlights, and

1938 Plymouth "Westchester" Suburban

Pontiac &Oakland

Pontiac Division, General Motors Corporation, Pontiac, Michigan

Pontiac is the only surviving GM "companion car." It's also the only GM nameplate introduced after 1908 that was still around after 1940. But during the early Depression, its future was nip-and-tuck. After Oakland had spawned the popular Pontiac Six in 1926, combined sales had soared, topping 200,000 units in 1929. But in the rock-bottom sales year of 1932, the division built less than 47,000 units, and lost a considerable amount of money. What saved Pontiac at this point was GM president Alfred Sloan's calm, confident management. In early 1933, Pontiac and Chevrolet manufacturing facilities were combined, saving vast amounts in tooling costs through the use of shared body components. At the same time, the Buick, Oldsmobile, and Pontiac sales organizations were consolidated: Dealers of each make were required to sell the other two as well. This belt-tightening measure remained in force through mid 1934, and in effect, it reduced GM to three divisions: Cadillac, Chevrolet, and B-O-P.

The well-styled 1933 Pontiac Straight Eight turned the marque's fortunes around. By 1937, Pontiac had exceeded the 200,000 mark again, and it remained among the top six producers through the end of the

1930 Pontiac Six rumble-seat convertible

1932 Pontiac Eight three-window coupe

decade. Pontiac was led in the 1930s by highly competent people: general manager William S. Knudsen, formerly from Ford; chief engineer Benjamin H. Anibal, father of the Pontiac eights; and Pontiac studio stylist Frank Hershey, creator of the stylish '33 and subsequent models.

Oakland, the parent nameplate, dated back as far as 1907, but had not sold well in the '20s. The Pontiac Six captured the majority of Oakland-Pontiac sales, with the result that the last Oaklands were produced in 1931. The 1930-31 Oaklands were all eight-cylinder cars riding a 117-inch wheelbase. Oakland roadsters, phaetons, and closed models were priced from $895 to $1055. The six-cylinder 1930-31 Pontiacs used 110-114-inch wheelbases and sold for $750-$850. Most of these were coupe and sedan models.

The 1930-31 Oakland V-8 engine, which was transferred to the Pontiac line for 1932, was a 250-cid 85-bhp unit created by Anibal. It had uncommon oversquare bore-and-stroke dimensions and an H-pattern cylinder head with the valves placed horizontally rather than parallel to the cylinders as in L-heads. Although the 1924 and later Cadillacs had featured ultra-smooth V-8s with 90-degree, heavily counterweighted crankshafts, the Oakland-Pontiac V-8 was an anachronism with its 180-degree crankshaft. This gave it teeth-chattering vibration above 2000 rpm, which the engineers tried to minimize with mixed results. The 180-degree crank made the Pontiac-Oakland V-8 cheaper to produce than the Cadillac's, but because it was not very smooth, this engine was superceded by an inline eight after a one-year run as a Pontiac series on the ex-Oakland 117-inch wheelbase.

Also an Anibal creation, the Pontiac Straight Eight of 1933 had 223.4 cid and 84 bhp. It was enlarged to 248.9 cid and 100 bhp in 1937, in which form it remained through 1939. Less square than the V-8, it was far more powerful, and quite smooth at high rpm. Highly reliable, it remained a staple of the larger Pontiacs all the way up through 1954.

During 1933 and 1934, eights were the only engines offered in Pontiacs as the division left sixes to Chevrolet. Though it was forced to share many Chevrolet body panels, Pontiac's designers were able to give their car a really different look. The two men chiefly responsible for this were Frank Hershey and chief body engineer Roy Milner. Hershey convinced GM styling head Harley Earl of the need for a more streamlined appearance in 1933, and accordingly designed a Bentley-type radiator as well as skirted front fenders with little "speed streaks." Milner gave the open models a smooth deck, and made their beltline moldings different from Chevrolet's. Combined with Pontiac's new "Knee-Action" independent front suspension and the new straight eight, the 1933 model was a highly pleasing package.

1933 Pontiac Eight convertible coupe

1935 Pontiac Six four-door sedan

1937 Pontiac Six convertible sedan

In performance, a Pontiac Straight Eight would not quite stay up with its Ford and Terraplane rivals, but the difference was insignificant. Pontiac's future was now assured.

With the economy looking up, a wider range of Pontiacs were fielded for 1935. A new 112-inch wheelbase carried two lines of smaller cars, the Standard and Deluxe Six. The L-head engine had 208 cubic inches and 80 horsepower. For 1937-39, the Six was enlarged to 222.8 cid and 85 bhp. The price difference between the Sixes and the Eights in 1935 was only about $100—but $100 then was like $500 now. Pontiac Sixes outsold Eights by a wide margin through the remainder of the decade.

Pontiac styling followed industry trends throughout the period. The 1930-32 models, including the Oaklands, were boxy, upright, and undistinguished. The 1933-34s, thanks to Hershey, were among the prettiest middle-priced automobiles of the era. In 1935, Pontiac inherited GM's all-steel "Turret Top" closed bodies, and originated its distinctive "Silver Streak"

styling motif. The "streak" started at the cowl and ran straight forward right over the hood and down the grille. It was originated by a young stylist named Virgil Exner, who would later contribute to the design of the postwar Studebakers and create Chrysler's "Forward Look" of the '50s. Exner liked chrome ornamentation, and his Silver Streak hallmark lasted for more than 20 years. Though the 1936-38 Pontiacs had massive horizontal grilles, the vertical streak was continued. The result was confused front-end styling which was cured in 1939 when Pontiacs acquired Harley Earl's "twin catwalk" grilles located between the fenders and main central grille. With all-vertical frontal lines, the '39 Pontiac looked much better than previous models. By this time, the car had also acquired smoother "pontoon" type fenders and lower body height.

Pontiac sales kept increasing through 1937. Calendar year figures were 175,000 units in 1935, 178,000 in 1936, and 235,000 cars in 1937. The 1938 recession cut production to only 95,000 cars and Pontiac dropped behind Dodge. But the next year, almost twice

1939 Pontiac Quality Deluxe Six two-door sedan

Pontiac & Oakland

as many Pontiacs rolled off the lines, and in 1940, Pontiac built a quarter-million vehicles for the first time. The division moved back into fifth place, a position it had not held since 1933.

Bill Knudsen decided on a two-series line for the 1937-38 model years. Six-cylinder wheelbases grew to 117 inches, eights to 122 inches. Except for a woody wagon on the six-cylinder chassis, body styles were identical: business coupe, sport coupe, cabriolet, two-door sedan and touring sedan, four-door sedan and touring sedan, and convertible sedan. The last, eliminated after 1938, was the nicest-looking Pontiac of these model years, as well as the most expensive. In 1938, it sold for $1310 with the six and $1358 with the eight. It was also the rarest body style of the period. Since the only time a convertible sedan was offered was 1937-38, this is among the most sought-after Pontiac models today.

As the recession eased in late 1938, Pontiac brought out a restyled 1939 line with three attractive series. Wheelbases were reduced by two inches for the Deluxe Eight and the former Deluxe Six, which was now called the "Quality Deluxe Six." A hybrid offering was the Deluxe 120, which used the six-cylinder engine on the 120-inch Deluxe Eight wheelbase. The Deluxe 120s and Deluxe Eights shared the same body styles: coupes, sedans, and a convertible. The Quality Deluxe, priced about $50 less than the 120, offered coupes, sedans, and a station wagon. There were no engine changes in 1939 and none appeared necessary. The Pontiac six was reliable and economical; the eight was smoother, perhaps a bit thirstier, but was certainly quite powerful. An English road test of a 1938 Eight suggested the car "might be borne along by the wind," so impressive were its quietness and smoothness.

Like all other companies, Pontiac would halt carmaking operations in early 1942 to convert to wartime production. After the war, it would rise to even greater heights than in the '30s with sales often running third behind Ford and Chevrolet. Pontiac's meteoric rise from near ruin in 1932 to profitability a year later and record sales in 1937 was due to sound management policies. But its formula for success, as the ads said in 1926, remained consistent and simple: "Give the Pontiac owner much of the luxury and comfort and fine detail of expensive cars at a price just dollars higher than the lowest-priced lines."

Pontiacs and Oaklands do not enjoy Classic status, but they have their admirers. The Pontiac-Oakland Club International, 3298 Maple Avenue, Allegeny, New York 14706, has 2000 members, a quarterly called *Silver Streak News,* and a monthly newsletter called *Smoke Signals.* Pontiac enthusiasts are interested in the early Oakland-built V-8s of 1930-32, and most agree that the Frank Hershey-styled 1933-34s with their straight-eight engines are the epitome of '30s motoring. Convertible sedans and other open cars of the later years are also sought after, yet prices of most 1930s Pontiacs remain relatively reasonable today.

photo credits: *Pontiac Motor Division, General Motors Corp.*

Reo

**Reo Motor Car Company,
Lansing, Michigan**

There was a difference of opinion at the Olds Motor Works in Lansing. Ransom Eli Olds, the founder, wanted nothing to do with four or six-cylinder automobiles; For him it was the single-cylinder "curved dash" Olds or nothing. His colleagues wanted to build more substantial cars, and they held a majority of the stock. The year was 1904.

Olds duly quit, set up a new company in the same Michigan town, named it Reo after his own initials (R.E.O.), and built more cars than Oldsmobile through 1917. The first Reos were single-cylinder runabouts, like Ransom's "Merry Oldsmobile." But gas was a dime a gallon in those days, and the trend was toward more powerful, much larger cars. Reo built fours through 1919 and sixes after 1920. There was even a companion make, Wolverine, in 1928 and 1929. After running third behind Ford and Buick in 1907, Reo gradually dropped in the production rankings. Its record year of 1923 saw over 30,000 units, but that was only good for a 14th place finish.

The Depression finished off Reo. After 11,450 cars in 1930, and 6800 for 1931, Reo never built more than 5000 cars a year. On the other hand, what it did build was memorable. The 1931 Royale was a pioneer streamlined design by Amos Northup—the first production automobile with fashionable skirted fenders. Royales of 1931, Royal Custom Eights of 1933, and the big 1932 8-35 and 8-52 models are all considered Classics today by the CCCA.

Reo used only L-head sixes in 1930. These were big powerplants sharing the same bore but with different strokes. The "Master" engine displaced 268.3 cid, had 80 bhp and was fitted in 121- to 124-inch-wheelbase chassis. The "Mate" was a 214.7-cid six with 60 bhp and mounted in a 115-inch-wheelbase chassis. In price, Reos were in the upper-middle bracket: The cheapest one you could buy in 1930 cost $1175; open models on the longer wheelbases could run as high as $1800. All Reos through mid 1931 were called Flying Clouds. The styling, by Northrup, was classic and formal. Flying Clouds showed a great sense of proportion, plus fine workmanship and quality interiors.

For 1931, the two sixes were joined by a 358-cid 125-bhp eight, mounted on a 130-inch wheelbase—the first of the Classic Reos. For "1931½" (the second '31 series), this model became the Series 8-31 Royale, and its wheelbase was 131 or 135 inches. In 1932, an immense 152-inch wheelbase model was added to the Royale family, and the car acquired enormous seven-passenger sedan and limousine bodies of substantial appearance. The 8-35 coupe, victoria, and five-passenger sedan sold for $2445 each; the long-wheelbase 8-52s listed at $3695-$3895, which was more than many Packards. The big nine-main-bearing straight eight made Royales effortless performers. But

they were the worst possible new products for a deepening Depression, and Reo sales fell by 50 percent in both 1931 and 1932.

Reo's management tried hard to economize. For the 1932½ season, beginning in January of that year, model offerings were drastically cut. A new 230-cid six with 80 bhp powered the 117-inch wheelbase Model 6-S. Listed were nine standard and deluxe closed and open body styles priced at $1000-$1200. The 6-S was a low-priced car and Reo's attempt to win back some of its lost business. The other two cars in the line were the Royale and Royale Custom, which shared the big 358-

1931 Reo Royale rumble-seat coupe

1933 Reo Royale Custom sedan

1933 Reo Royale Custom sedan

1934 Reo Royale Custom sedan

Reo

cid engine. Royales used the 131-inch wheelbase, Customs the 135- and 152-inch versions. The same line was offered for 1933, with the engine for the 6-S bored out to 268 cid for 85 bhp. The company continued its practice of mid-year revisions in January 1933, but the changes were slight. The 152-inch wheelbase was eliminated from the eight-cylinder line, which now consisted of the Royale Standard, Elite, and Custom. Prices were cut at the same time, though the reductions were not large enough to matter much. Reo registrations totaled only 3623 for 1933, the worst year on record.

Reo brought out most of its 1934 models in July and September of 1933. The Flying Cloud S-2/S-3, the Royale Eight N-2, the Custom Royale Eight N-1 were all carried over from 1933 with only minor changes. It wasn't until April that Reo introduced a "genuine" '34, the Model S-4 Flying Cloud. This lovely car featured smooth, streamlined styling with a new grille and hood, hood side louvers, deeper skirted fenders, and an optional built-in trunk for the four-door sedans. The S-4 had the same basic bodies and 268-cid six of previous Flying Clouds and the same 117-inch wheelbase. Unfortunately, it was no more successful. Reo production

for calendar year 1934 was only 4460 cars, plus 11,222 trucks.

The debut of the S-4 was overshadowed by internal company quarrels which had been erupting sporadically since the Wall Street crash. Ransom E. Olds was still hanging in there during the early '30s but his resignation in December, 1933 caused a management crisis and in April, 1934, Donald E. Bates was elected president. Olds returned briefly to the board, and Reo continued the 4-S as the 1935 Model S-5.

On January 2, 1935, a brand new Flying Cloud marked the "1935½" season. This was an ambitious restyle offering fastback two-door and four-door sedan bodies. The wheelbase was 115 inches, while the engine had 228 cid and 90 bhp. Reo's front-end revamp somewhat resembled that of the 1935 Auburn with flared fenders and a V-shaped bumper. Ransom Olds was against this new Flying Cloud, claiming that the $450,000 spent in tooling it was wasted: In his mind, the '34 was fine as it was.

But, as in years past at Oldsmobile, the rest of Reo management disagreed. They pushed ahead with bigger changes for 1936: the Model 6-D/E/F/G Flying Cloud. These cars were much more substantial looking than their predecessors. They had fuller fenders, a reworked grille and hood, vertical grille bands that wrapped up over the radiator shell, rubber-tipped bumper guards, and optional "Zeppelin-style" fender lamps. There was no self-shifter option, but in May, 1936, Reo did announce an optional overdrive.

Cars, however, were a sideline by now, and only Reo's trucks were profitable. The new Flying Cloud sold no better than earlier models: The company built a mere 3206 cars in 1936, versus 4692 in 1935. Another '35 model was the 6-7S Royale, but this was merely a '34 with a revised grille and hood louvers. A pathetic end for the mighty Royale, this car was retained as the Model 6-75 for 1936.

On May 18, 1936, the Reo board approved moving truck assembly into the main plant; on September 3rd, the automobile business ended. Reo lost nearly $1.4 million on the '36s, of which $604,000 was a write-off charge for ending car production. But the company

1934 Reo S-4 Flying Cloud convertible coupe

1936 Reo 6-D Flying Cloud sedan

1936 Reo 6-D Flying Cloud sedan

1935 Reo 6-A Flying Cloud sedan

1937 Reo Speed Delivery panel truck

managed to survive as a truck builder for almost 40 years. Reo became a division of White Trucks in 1957 which combined Reo operations with Diamond T as the Diamond-Reo Division in 1967. In 1971, Reo became independent again, and after ending production temporarily in 1975, the firm is now a division of the Osterlund Company and is still producing trucks.

One chance for survival as a car maker was missed, however. A plan for a joint Reo-Graham operation was placed before the Reo board by Graham-Paige officials in July, 1935. The Reo people balked, fearing a loss of independence. They did let Graham use the Flying Cloud body for Graham's 1936-37 line but that was as far as cooperation progressed. A Reo-Graham merger would have made a lot of sense. Both cars could have used the same body, built in Graham's Dearborn plant, while Reo built trucks in Lansing. A joint dealer body would have minimized sales costs. And the Graham brothers knew the truck business—they had built the Dodge truck operation before founding their own com-

pany in 1927. Unfortunately, the combination never had a chance. Thus, the Reo and Graham nameplates both vanished before World War II.

Except for the high-priced, Classic-rated Royale Eights, Reos remain good buys for collectors today. The Flying Clouds led American design in the early '30s and were considered good-looking machines in 1934. The 1935 range includes some of the most interesting sedans in the "potato period" of mid '30s styling: the 6-A models with their crisp fastbacks, and the 7-S with its blend of '20s and '30s design elements. Flying Cloud Sixes in excellent condition have changed hands recently for as little as $3500, and restorable mid-decade models have been advertised for only $1000 and up. The marque is served by the Reo Club of America, Rt. 2, Box 190, Forest, Ohio 45843.

photo credits: Special Interest Autos *Magazine; Reo Club of America, Inc.; Ray Courtad; Ray M. Wood*

Studebaker, Erskine & Rockne

**Studebaker Corporation,
South Bend, Indiana**

The oldest manufacturer of wheeled vehicles in the 1930s, Studebaker had been around since brothers Henry and Clem joined to build three covered wagons in 1852. All five Studebaker brothers—each of them as bearded as the Brothers Smith—participated in the affairs of the firm over the years. J. M. "Wheelbarrow Johnny" Studebaker was running the company in 1902, when it began building automobiles. Through 1910, Studebaker built only electrics, as "Mr. J. M." hated gas-powered cars. He called them "clumsy, dangerous, noisy brutes [which] stink to high heaven, break down at the worst possible moment, and are a

1930 Erskine Six brougham

1932 Rockne convertible coupe

1931 Studebaker Dictator Eight sedan

public nuisance." But even John Studebaker bowed to the inevitability of the gasoline engine in 1911.

J. M. Studebaker relinquished the presidency to Albert Russell Erskine in 1915, and it was this former accountant who took Studebaker into the '30s. The company had prospered before the Depression. In 1922, for example, Studebaker built over 100,000 cars and ranked right up with industry leaders Ford, Chevrolet, Dodge, and Buick. Then, Erskine took over and made a series of mistakes, beginning with the car he named after himself, the Erskine Six which appeared in 1924. By 1930, its engine displaced 160 cubic inches, and had 70 bhp. Though comparable in design, (except for the number of cylinders) to the Model A Ford, the Erskine's $1000 price was double the Model A's, and the car was ultimately a failure. It was dropped after 1930.

Erskine made other mistakes, too. He bought Pierce-Arrow in 1928, just before the Wall Street crash that would make life almost unliveable for luxury-car builders. In the depths of the Depression, 1932-33, Erskine put Studebaker's smallest six-cylinder engine into a separate make, the Rockne, named in honor of South Bend's favorite football coach, Knute Rockne. Of course, anyone who didn't follow Notre Dame football was at a loss to identify with the name. Rocknes came in two models: a 189.8-cid Six on a 110-inch wheelbase; and a 205.3-cid Six on a 114-inch wheelbase. Though its price, at $600-$700, was far more reasonable than the Erskine's, the Rockne failed to penetrate a market dominated by long-established makes. It was dropped in 1934, and its larger six-cylinder powerplant was pushed up to 88 bhp for Studebaker's Dictator Six. The Dictator was another bizarre moniker of the Erskine presidency. It was one of Studebaker's series names which included associated titles like Commander and President. After Hitler and Mussolini came to power, a name like Dictator was downright un-American. Yet incredibly, Studebaker stayed with it through 1937.

Not counting the Erskine, Studebaker fielded no less than six different engines and models for 1930, which suggests clearly that the Depression caught A. R. Erskine totally by surprise. There were Dictator and Commander Sixes and Eights, the Dictators on a 115-inch wheelbase, Commanders on a 120-inch span. Studebaker tried offering six and eight-cylinder engines of comparable size and power. The capacity of both Dictator engines was 221 cid, the eight producing 70 bhp and the six 68 bhp. The Commander six had 248.3 cid and 75 bhp, the Commander eight 250.4 cid and 80 bhp.

Bracketing the Dictators and Commanders was the 205.3-cid Studebaker Six built on the 114-inch wheelbase of the 1932-33 Rockne, and the top-of-the-line President Eight. The President was a magnificent car, mounted on a 125-or 135-inch wheelbase. Through 1933, it carried a potent straight eight of 337 cubic inches. Though not considered Classic cars, these were certainly classic Studebakers—the finest automobiles South Bend built during the decade, and perhaps the finest ever. Studebaker said that the President "finds a parallel in sustained speed only in the light of comets, meteors and other heavenly bodies." Such unabashed hyperbole was based on a stellar performance demonstrated in the 1928 announcement year. Two totally stock President Eight roadsters had each traveled over 30,000 miles in less than 27,000 minutes.

In proportion, the President was immense: Wheelbases ranged up to 137 inches. In pedigree, it was impressive. The engineer responsible for it was two-fisted, hard-driving Delmar G. "Barney" Roos, previously of Locomobile, Marmon, and Pierce-Arrow. Though large, beautiful, and quite fast, the car sold at modest prices—as little as $1625.

Heart of the President was Roos' short-stroke eight, which displaced 337 cubic inches in its 1930s form. The block and crankcase were integrally cast, and the engine turned only 2800 rpm at 60 mph. For 1930, the President engine produced 115 bhp. The next year it was given nine (instead of five) main bearings, a coated-steel crankshaft, and higher compression, all of which boosted output to 122 bhp. This rose to 132 bhp for 1933. The crank was derived from the Liberty aircraft engine, and was largely responsible for the President's tremendous low-end stamina.

Economic misfortunes caused the demise of the big-inch Presidents after 1933, but not before they had written a great racing story. President-derived racing

1931 Studebaker President Eight touring

cars competed with distinction at Indianapolis, for example. Russel Snowberger drove them to eighth and fifth place in 1930 and 1931, averaging over 90 mph. The factory sent a team to Indy in 1932, and a car driven by Cliff Bergere finished third with an average speed of 102.66 mph. This was the first time a semi-stock car had exceeded the 100-mph mark. In 1933, Tony Gulotta ended the factory's Indy campaign by finishing seventh at 99 mph.

Studebaker model offerings were drastically cut in 1931. The Erskine was dropped, along with all Studebaker sixes except the small 205-cid unit. Eights comprised Dictator, Commander, and President versions ranging in output from 70 to 122 bhp, and in wheelbase from 114 to 136 inches. The same lineup continued in 1932-33, when the 205 six went into the Rockne. Studebaker also retained a six for its own line, a 230-cid 80-bhp engine for the 117-inch-wheelbase Dictator chassis. In 1934, with the end of the Rockne, the 205 sixes came flooding back into Studebaker's Standard, Special, and Deluxe Dictators, all rated at 88 bhp.

Though all auto companies suffered during the early

1932 Studebaker President Eight rumble-seat roadster

Studebaker, Erskine & Rockne

'30s, Studebaker suffered more than most. The successive failures of the Erskine, Pierce-Arrow, and Rockne were accompanied by profligate financial practices. For instance, Studebaker continued to pay dividends through 1931, even though the money had to come from the firm's capital reserves. The company tried to merge with White Motors, but the deal fell through. Sales slowly dwindled. Production was 52,000 cars in 1930, 49,000 in '31, 44,000 in '32, and 43,000 in '33—not enough to break even. In 1933, Studebaker went into receivership and Erskine resigned, only to die shortly afterwards by his own hand.

Studebaker was saved at this point by production vice-president Harold S. Vance and sales vice-president Paul G. Hoffman, the two men who would jointly guide the company's destiny through 1949. Vance and Hoffman rid Studebaker of Pierce-Arrow and started up South Bend's idle production lines. In mid 1934, the firm realized a small profit, but it was enough to secure a line of credit. The corner had been turned. Production now began to inch up: 46,000 units in 1934, 49,000 in 1935. In 1936-37, volume was up over the 80,000 level.

Under Vance and Hoffman, Erskine's full-line market approach was reversed. For the 1935 model year, Studebaker fielded only three series, the Dictator Six, Commander Eight, and President Eight, with wheelbases of 114, 120, and 124 inches respectively. The Dictator used the 205-cid six, while the Commander and President shared a 100-plus-bhp, 250-cid eight which had been around since 1930. For 1936-37, the Commander line was dropped and Studebaker concentrated solely on medium-priced, cleanly styled Dic-

tators and Presidents. The former's engines were bored out to 217.8 cid, which yielded 90 bhp and the output of the President engine was increased to 115. Both models also had longer wheelbases.

Studebaker styling through the decade was usually good and sometimes exceptional. The formal lines of the early years gave way in 1933 to graceful skirted fenders and radiators that curved forward at the bottom. In the streamlined period of the mid '30s, Studebakers adopted pontoon fenders and rounded grilles like most other cars, but retained a crisp, individual appearance. Mid-decade also saw technical progress. Along with Warner overdrive in 1935, Studebaker offered Barney Roos' novel "planar" independent front suspension. This successful innovation consisted of a transverse leaf spring with upper and lower links, and rotary (or later telescopic) shocks. The next year, Studebaker was trumpeting its new "Hill Holder," a coupling between the clutch and brake system which prevented a car from rolling backward down hills when the clutch was disengaged. Other new features of the mid '30s were automatic choke, vacuum-powered brakes, rotary door latches, and all-steel bodies. Most of these were Barney Roos' doing, though he had left Studebaker for Britain's Rootes Group in 1936. Roos later returned to America and Willys-Overland, where he participated in the design of the World War II Jeep. His place at Studebaker was taken by W. S. James, but the real engineering power after Roos' departure was Roy Cole, vice-president of engineering.

To restyle the 1938 models, Paul Hoffman brought in brilliant industrial designer Raymond Loewy, who had impressed him with the beautifully styled 1932-34 Hupmobiles. In short order, Studebakers began to look exceptionally good. Loewy gave the cars a prow-front motif with flush-mounted headlights in 1938, one year before most competitors. Studebaker's Zephyr-like front end in 1939 imitated the streamlined Lincoln, but the result was a very pretty and distinctive look. Also in

1935 Studebaker Commander Eight two-door coupe

1938 Studebaker President Eight four-door sedan

1939 Studebaker Champion Custom coupe

1939 Studebaker Commander Six sedan

1938, Studebaker dropped the Dictator name and resurrected the Commander. Production faltered at 46,000 during this recession year, but in 1939, it improved thanks to the new economy Champion. The Champ was just what South Bend needed. Production hit 106,470 cars for 1939, a record for the decade and the company's best year since 1928.

The cleanly styled Champion succeeded because of its price and performance. At $660-$800, it cost about the same as a Chevy or Ford and less than most Plymouths. Its 164.3-cid 78-bhp L-head six was smaller and less powerful than "Big Three" engines, but the Champion also weighed 500-700 pounds less than its rivals. This allowed it to deliver comparable performance and fantastic gas mileage—up to 22 mpg. The Champion was no match for the 85-bhp Ford V-8, but it would run up to 78 mph—equal to or better than Chevy, Plymouth, and the 60-bhp Ford.

The 11,000-member Studebaker Drivers Club (Box 3044, South Bend, Indiana 46619) honors all Studebaker, Erskine, and Rockne cars, and covers the whole span of the company's products from 1902-66.

Among Studebaker enthusiasts, there is no question about the most desirable model of the '30s: It's the 1930-33 President Eight, even though it's now priced out of reach for all but the very wealthy. Some Studebaker enthusiasts voice pleasure at the fact that the President doesn't enjoy Classic status, for if it did, prices would be that much higher. Among other outstanding Studebakers of the 1930s are the smoothly styled 1933-34 models, graceful transitions between the boxy shapes of the '20s and the streamlined designs of the late '30s. Post-1933 Presidents were still the top-of-the-line, but were far cries indeed from their predecessors. Model year 1939 represents a styling renaissance for Studebaker, as well as its best sales year of the decade. The '39s are, therefore, among the more desirable of the period. Among body styles, convertible sedans and the elegant "Four Season" roadsters are the most prized.

photo credits: *Richard Quinn*

Stutz

Stutz Motor Car Company of America, Indianapolis, Indiana

Mention Stutz and most people immediately conjure up an image of the fabulous Bearcat piloted at breathtaking speeds along a country lane by a raccoon-coated playboy. Or they think of Harry K. Stutz, the founder, and his "car that made good in a day." There were Stutz Bearcats in the '30s, too, but they were rather different from the dashing speedsters of the '10s. They were also products of a different genius: Frederick E. Moskovics.

Though Moskovics left the company in 1929, Stutzes of the 1930s were very much his own. European-born, brilliantly educated, financially comfortable, Moskovics was socially at ease in any company. Round faced, amply proportioned, and usually found smoking an expensive cigar, he looked every inch the genial tycoon he was—especially when dressed in plus-fours and golfing cap. A keen racing enthusiast, he had managed the Mercedes Vanderbilt Cup team. He took it for granted that the desirable lessons of the race track should be built into production automobiles.

Moskovics was typically American in his fascination with the march of technological progress. He delighted in the finer European sporting machines, but he scorned the idea that such cars must be slowly and expensively hand-built. He saw that technical know-how could be harnessed to produce a thoroughbred machine at reasonable cost. And that is what he created: an American thoroughbred. Like Fred Duesenberg, Fred Moskovics was not interested in or given to compromise. There was only one right way, and he found it every time.

The 1930s were the last years for this great marque, and there were no major mechanical changes from 1930 through the last Stutz cars of 1936. The Vertical Eight, introduced four years earlier, was the basis for all models, except the notorious 1929-30 Blackhawk with its Continental L-head eight.

The Depression killed Stutz, but its sporting image didn't help the company, either. Stutz was handily outsold by Cadillac, Packard, Lincoln, and Pierce-Arrow because the luxury-car buyer demanded silence, riding comfort, mechanical simplicity, reliability, and ease of maintenance. These were hard to achieve in a machine capable of being raced successfully as it stood on the showroom floor. A Stutz speedster could out-run all but the Model J Duesenberg. Yet, Stutz sedans, with their relatively low rear axle ratios, were buzz boxes below 50 mph, despite their silence above that speed. The lack of crankshaft counterweights was questionable in a high-revving engine, though they would have further increased the engine's already complex servicing requirements.

The 1930 Stutz Model M Vertical Eight used a 322-cid engine (called the SV-16) with 115 bhp. Its power-per-cubic-inch figure was outstanding, its rpm capability higher than similarly sized engines, but its power-per-pound ratio was mediocre. More displacement would have compensated for the car's weight and a higher final drive would have increased engine life and fuel economy, but 322 cubic inches was as large as the Stutz engine would ever get. In bhp rating it was outclassed by the multi-cylinder engines of Cadillac, Lincoln, Auburn, Packard, Marmon, and Pierce. Stutz could not afford to retool for engines of 12 or 16 cylinders, though the company did experiment with a supercharger, which boosted the Eight's horsepower from 113 to 143. The blower was a huge affair, mounted low in front of the radiator and driven directly from the crankshaft. It did the job, but it was noisy, and carburetion was a problem.

For 1931, Stutz followed Duesenberg's approach and designed a new 32-valve head with dual overhead camshafts. The dual ignition system of the SV-16 engine was lost in the process (there was no room for it).

1930 Stutz DV-32 Monte Carlo sedan

1931 Stutz DV-32 sport sedan by Weymann

1931 Stutz DV-32 coupe by Waterhouse

1931 Stutz convertible sedan by Waterhouse

1932 Stutz DV-32 coupe by Waterhouse

1931 Stutz Bearcat torpedo speedster

Improved breathing gave the new DV-32 some 156 bhp at 3900 rpm.

Stutzes were expensive. The SV-16 sold for $2995-$3995 in 1931-32. The DV-32 started at a minimum of $3995 and usually cost $5000 or more: The chassis alone cost $3200. Stutz offered about 30 body styles by such leading coachbuilders as LeBaron, Fleetwood, Rollston, Weymann, Brunn, Waterhouse, and Derham. Weymann's unusual fabric bodies were made of padded leatherette. Compared to steel bodies they were light, strong, safe, elastic, quiet, and durable. They soaked up road shock and noise, lasted longer, and were easier to repair. Because the color was impregnated in the lacquer-coated cloth, these bodies never faded or needed repainting. But many people disliked the dull pebbled finish and dowdy looks. Another novel body was the aluminum Monte Carlo sedan, selling for a stratospheric $8995. Not surprisingly, only three ever left the factory.

For 1931, Stutz also offered the six-cylinder Model LA, which was designated the LAA for 1932-33. As an attempt to cut prices against the deepening Depression, the 1931 LA sedan listed for only $2245, and the

1932 LAA for $1645. In reality, the engine of these cars was a Vertical Eight minus two cylinders. At over 4300 pounds, these were hardly performance cars and fewer than 50 LAA Stutzes found buyers.

The DV-32 Stutz was shown in chassis form at the New York Auto Show in the winter of 1930-31. By the end of March, 1931, the factory had announced prices, and by July, the DV-32 was in production. At the same time, Stutz announced it had netted $20,000 as of July 31 on a gross profit of $100,000. That was a pitifully meager income, but better than the red ink which had been flowing since 1929. The DV-32 was demonstrated in dramatic fashion across the country as three groups of cars, called "flying circuses," toured the nation. They were led by a new model with an old name: Bearcat. This romantic design, a late addition to the DV-32 line, was calculated to stir up nostalgic feelings among potential customers. A "Super Bearcat" had a special 116-inch wheelbase and was initially fitted with Weymann bodies covered with artificial leather.

With a 4.1:1 rear axle ratio, the standard Stutz was capable of 90 mph. The Super Bearcat was guaran-

Stutz

teed to do 100-plus mph. Stutz sedans could be cruised at 60 or even 70 mph; they would reach 25 mph in first gear, 48 in second, and 70 in third. First gear was actually an emergency ratio. It could be engaged only by lifting a lockout device on the lever of the four-speed gearbox, which had been introduced in 1929 along with the 322-cid engine.

Stutz brakes were hydraulic with servo-vacuum assist, and could be adjusted from a control on the instrument panel. A one-shot central lubrication system meant that only three points required lubrication—the water pump bearings and the distributor. Semi-elliptic springs and hydraulic shock absorbers provided suspension. Final drive was by worm gear which had originally appeared on the "Safety Stutz" chassis in 1926.

For 1932, Stutz announced several changes. The original four-speed transmission was replaced with a very rugged, synchronized three-speed Muncie unit, and free-wheeling was now an option. The hot-air manifold was replaced with a hot-water heating system, and an oil cooler was provided for the engine. A new trunk rack and dust valance were installed in the rear and the body dropped in a curving line to cover the straight frame. Single-bar bumpers replaced the original double bars. The 115-bhp SV-16 Stutz engine was continued along with the DV-32.

When Indianapolis regulations were relaxed in 1930 to allow stock-car based entries, Stutz made a point of running *strictly* stock to add a touch of drama to its track appearances. Thus, the 1930 Indianapolis "Jones Special" was powered by the 322 engine. This car used the highest optional gear ratio (3.6:1), and at the 500 it averaged 85.35 mph. Stutz was the only stock car in the race, and therefore weighed 1500 pounds more than the next heaviest car. Despite this burden, it finished in tenth place—one of the great stock-car performances of all time.

Also in 1930, Stutz entered the 24-hour race at Le-Mans. The LeMans single-cam engines were identical to the one used in the Indianapolis car. Its performance was at an all-time high, but the car didn't seem to have enough speed to lead the race—at least not in the opening laps. "Big car" competition was fierce: the 38-250 seven-liter Mercedes and the Bentley 6.5 liter. The Stutz entries would have needed a supercharger boost of 8-10 pounds to equal their competitors' speed, but Stutz had lost interest in blowers and was perfecting the DV-32. The race began in a state of bedlam. With the whine of the Mercedes supercharger, and the harsh scream of tires as the Bentley was flung about with appalling regularity, new record times were being set almost every lap and the atmosphere was charged with excitement. Stutz driver Edward Brisson spent three hours working his car up to fifth place behind the lead Mercedes and the three fastest Bent-

leys. Then, his co-driver Louis Rigal took over. Rigal tore out of the pits and almost immediately ran off the road, ripping loose the car's exhaust system. Shortly afterward, the Stutz caught fire and retired.

But the company hadn't finished with the 1930 season. In September, a Stutz won the Mexican road race between Nuevo Laredo and Monterey, a distance of 140 miles. Cecil Bixby, in the stock-car event, won with an elapsed time of one hour, 56 minutes—two minutes ahead of a Studebaker Commander Eight. His average speed was 70.71 mph. In November, E. G. "Cannonball" Baker broke the transcontinental trip record in a Stutz Weymann sedan covering 3220 miles in 68 hours and 51 minutes for an average of 52.92 mph. This bettered the old time by nearly seven hours and also beat the quickest train time by 15 hours. Meanwhile, in France, Brisson won the 8-liter class in his Bearcat at the Gometz le Chatel hillclimb. Brisson gave Stutz a final fling at LeMans in 1932, but retired after colliding with an Alfa Romeo.

During 1932, Stutz lost $315,000, but continued to stumble on. In 1933, the firm lost close to a half-million dollars; in 1934, it lost a quarter-million. While not large amounts by standards of the day, these losses were tremendous drains on the company's meager resources.

A partial recovery was sought through sales of a line of small trucks called Pak-Age-Cars. George H. Freers was appointed chief engineer in charge of Pak-Age-Car activities. In the summer of 1936, the first 28 of these Stutz-built delivery vehicles were completed out of a total order of 340. This was not enough to keep Stutz going but the firm filed a bankruptcy petition in April, 1937. By this time, total assets were $1.2 million, liabilities only $733,000, but the firm could not meet its debts. In April, 1938, a federal judge ordered liquidation of all assets, since the creditors could not agree upon a reorganization plan. In the summer of 1938, all Stutz assets were sold and the Pak-Age-Car idea was absorbed by the Diamond T Truck Company.

It seems almost superfluous to mention that the Classic Car Club of America considers every Stutz of the '30s a Classic, or that the cars command staggering prices on today's collector markets. The most recent recorded price for a Stutz—an SV-16—was $82,000. Although that may be extreme, the even more desirable DV-32 in prime condition is certainly going to cost a king's ransom—at least on the rare occasion when one comes up for sale. Like the Duesenberg, and to some extent the Marmon, Stutz was a car apart. Shunning the likes of all-out luxury machines like Packard and Pierce-Arrow, Fred Moskovics built hairy performers, as much at home on a twisty road course as on a paved highway. In Ken Purdy's words, they were the kind of cars "that used the power normally apportioned to a couple of trucks to carry two passengers in utter glory."

---

photo credits: *Motor Vehicle Manufacturers Association*

Willys, Overland, Whippet

Willys-Overland Motors, Toledo, Ohio

John North Willys was a car dealer in Elmira, New York with a yen to do more than just sell the things. In 1907, he bought the ailing Overland Company of Indianapolis. A year later, he renamed it Willys-Overland, moved into the old Pope plant in Toledo, Ohio, and began to rebuild its fortunes. For most of the '10s, the four-cylinder Overland was second only to the Model T Ford in sales, and by 1918, J. N. Willys owned the second largest auto company in the world. The post-World War I recession slowed production, but in 1926, Willys-Overland announced the low-priced Whippet and sales soared. The all-time record came in 1928, when Toledo built 315,000 cars and rocketed to third place behind Chevrolet and Ford. Then came the Depression which knocked the company for a loop. In 1933, Willys-Overland declared bankruptcy. Production was resumed after reorganization, but in calendar year 1934, the company built only about 8000 cars.

The Toledo-built cars entered the '30s with a name change: The Overland badge was dropped in favor of the Willys nameplate. The price leaders were the Whippets, which came in two versions: a 40-bhp, 145.7-cid four on a 103-inch wheelbase; and a 50-bhp, 178.3-cid six on a 112.5-inch wheelbase. Though the Whippet Four was priced as low as $505, sales had already seen the best days. Sales through 1931 were dismal, and the Whippet was dropped for 1932.

Willys-Overland also offered the sleeve-valve Willys-Knight from 1930 through 1933. J. N. Willys got into this act in 1916, when he launched the powerplant which bore his own name. The W-K engine employed that interesting valve arrangement patented by the brilliant inventor Charles Yale Knight. Instead of conventional cam-and-spring-actuated poppet valves, Knight conceived of a double sliding sleeve which let the fuel-air mixture directly into the cylinders. Many makes used sleeve-valved engines in the '10s, but Willys built more of them than anybody else, and con-

1931 Willys Eight Deluxe Victoria coupe

1927 Whippet sedan ('30/ '31 models similar)

1932 Willys Six three-window coupe

Willys, Overland, Whippet

tinued them longer. Though Knight's system was very advanced compared to its early contemporaries, it was also highly complicated. The simple, efficient side-valve engine was more practical, and found favor even on luxury makes like Cadillac.

Willys-Knights of the early '30s were six-cylinder models offered in two sizes. The smaller versions used 112.5 to 115-inch wheelbases with a 178-cid engine and 55 bhp. They sold in 1930-31 for around $1000. The larger Knight was offered through 1933, at up to $1895. It used a 255-cid six with 72 to 87 horsepower, and 120- or 121-inch wheelbases. The '33 Streamline Six, sold only in sedan form for $1420, was the last sleeve-valve car built in America.

The rest of Willys' line in the early '30s was comprised of conventional L-head sixes and eights. A 193-cid six with 65 bhp came as a roadster, sedan or coupe. Styling was attractive, as were the prices, which ranged from $500 to $800. The Willys Eight used a

longer wheelbase; its engine displaced 245 cubic inches and yielded a creditable 80 bhp. The Eight was introduced in 1931—an inopportune time for big-engined cars. Bankruptcy finished off both the Six and the Eight in early 1933.

The reorganization following bankruptcy proceedings brought bespectacled Ward Canaday to the Willys-Overland helm. A pillar of the Toledo business community with a great sense of loyalty to his men, Canaday ached to get the corporation back on its feet. Under his management, all of Willys-Overland's resources were put into a new small car built on a 100-inch wheelbase, the Willys 77. Continued with little change from early 1933 through 1936, the 77 was the sole Willys model. Its ultra-economical 134.2-cid four developed 48 bhp. Styling was unique, and unmistakable: The radiator was hidden under the hood. A vertical-bar grille, round at the top, tapered to a sharp point at the bottom. The grille's shape, and its forward pitch at the bottom, earned this Willys the derisive nickname of "potato digger." Living up to the title, it dug a financial hole in the ground. The best production Willys was able to achieve was 20,428 cars in calendar year 1935. Today, the 77's shape looks refreshing compared to most of the lumpy cars of this era. But in the '30s—

1932 Willys Eight Custom sedan

1937 Willys Model 36 standard sedan

1932 Willys Six roadster

1936 Willys Model 77 coupe

1938 Willys Model 38 Deluxe sedan

despite prices as low as $395—it just wouldn't sell.

For 1937, Canaday had another idea. Retaining the "potato digger's" 48-bhp engine and 100-inch wheelbase, he had the car fully restyled. The result was—again—less than ideal. A rounded body with pontoon fenders was headed by a wild front end, not unlike that of the sharknose Graham. Standard and Deluxe coupes and sedans were offered at $500-$600. The car was called the Model 36, then Model 38 in 1938, and finally 38 and 48 for 1939. While the styling of this series was no less bizarre than the Willys 77's, it met with some success. Sales shot up to 76,803 in 1937. But this was a recovery year for the whole industry: Despite tripled production, Willys was only able to move from 15th to 14th place in the industry. The recession of 1938 put output back to 16,173, and Willys slipped to 15th place again.

For 1939, Toledo fielded the same weird-looking line as in the previous two years and they sold just a little better than the '38s. What helped was a revived Overland, on a 102-inch wheelbase, which was styled differently than the Willys. It had a very Graham-like front end, but instead of that car's flush-mounted headlamps, the Overland's were carried in clumsy fender pods. Overland prices, at $600-$650, were just a little higher than Willys, but the extra money bought significantly better performance. With a compression increase and a fixed-jet carburetor, engineers had coaxed 62 bhp out of the Willys four-cylinder engine. Calendar year production moved up to 25,383 units.

In 1939, Joseph W. Frazer left Chrysler Corporation to become president and general manager of Willys-Overland, while Canaday remained board chairman. When it came to sales, Joe Frazer knew how to cut his losses. Conventional styling was ordained for 1940, and the patriotic model name "American" arrived in 1941. However, it's doubtful even Frazer could have saved Willys passenger cars. The company's salvation, ultimately, was the wartime Jeep.

Willys cars of the '30s have a collector standing today which reflects their mixed reviews when new. None are Classics, and none except for the technically interesting Willys-Knight are really memorable for their historic significance. Knights are welcomed by the Willys-Overland-Knight Registry, 241 Orchard Drive, Dayton, Ohio 45419. All post-1933 Willys cars are covered by the Willys Club, 137 Plymouth Avenue, Oreland, Pennsylvania 19075.

---

photo credits: *Motor Vehicle Manufacturers Association*

1939 Willys Model 48 sedan

1939 Willys Model 48 club coupe

1939 Willys Model 48 sedan

Minor Makes

The 1930s were full of American makes and companies other than those on the preceding pages, most of which were finished off by the prevailing Depression. Some of them had ventured into making passenger cars in an attempt to salvage what was left of their fortunes; some were remnants of once great companies; others were independents without the financial protection of a GM or a Ford or a Chrysler. A few, like Jordan, duPont, Kissel, and Mercer, were cars that had inspired the imagination of Americans in years past. And the loss of those makes, in particular, was regrettable.

BREWSTER
Springfield Manufacturing Company, Springfield, Massachusetts
This was an attempt in 1934 to salvage some business for what was left of the Brewster Coachbuilding company. Special bodies, sometimes open, but more usually closed, were placed on Ford, Buick, and other chassis, but the cars used Brewster nameplates. About 300 were sold for very high prices—$3000 and up—before the effort foundered in 1936.

CONTINENTAL
Continental Automobile Company, Detroit, Michigan
The famous independent engine company fielded four and six-cylinder cars under its own name in 1933, based on the uninspiring body styles of DeVaux, which by then was out of business. The fours sold for as little as $335, and used a 101.5-inch wheelbase; the Light Six and Ace Big Six had 65- and 85-bhp engines, and used 107- and 114-inch wheelbases. Fours only were offered in 1934, the make's second and last year.

CROSLEY
Crosley Motors, Inc., Richmond, Indiana
Radio and refrigerator magnate Powel Crosley, Jr. entered the minicar field in 1939 when he built his first cars which had an 80-inch wheelbase. The original idea was to sell Crosleys through hardware or appliance shops, but conventional dealerships soon sprang up. The '39 models comprised a convertible coupe for two ($325) and a convertible sedan for four ($350). A total of 1200 were built. The '39 engine was an air-cooled twin with just 12 horsepower. Crosley went on to modest success after the war, selling a record 29,000 cars in 1948, but the firm was out of the car business by 1952.

CUNNINGHAM
James Cunningham and Sons Company, Rochester, New York
One of the most expensive, luxurious automobiles built in America, the Cunningham was produced through 1933 by a 100-year old company. Its 355-cid V-8 produced 110 bhp in 1930. Posh open and closed bodies were built mostly by Cunningham itself. The works even supplied bodies for other premium chassis in 1931. By 1932, the V-8 was up to a rather impressive 140 bhp, and Cunningham was concentrating on the longer 142-inch wheelbase. With prices as high as $9000, the firm found few buyers. After 1933, Cunningham dropped its own cars and built bodies for other manufacturers. One of these, like a comparable Brewster, was mated to a Ford V-8 chassis. It was a town car and sold for $2600—about 4½ times more expensive than the basic Ford sedan. Cunningham also built hearses and ambulances on Packard, Cadillac, and Lincoln chassis before it closed business in 1936. All Cunningham V-8 cars have Classic status.

DE VAUX
De Vaux-Hall Motor Corp., Grand Rapids, Michigan
In 1931, most auto makers were thinking about leaving the car business, not *entering* it. But Norman De Vaux, president of Durant of California, felt he could do what others could not. De Vaux was incorporated in February, 1931. It was bankrupt by April, 1932.

De Vaux used a Continental L-head six of 214.7 cid and 70 bhp to power his model 6-75, which had a 113-inch wheelbase and a price range of $645-$885. Its successor, the model 6-80 for 1932, listed slightly higher. After De Vaux went broke, this model was marketed as the "Continental De Vaux" by the Continental company. In 1933, the same basic cars were again marketed under the Continental nameplate. De Vaux production was 4315 cars for model year 1931 and 1239 units for 1932.

duPONT
duPont Motors Inc., Moore, Pennsylvania
E. Paul duPont's superlative Classics were among the finest luxury cars of the era. Like many marques of similar high calibre, it too was condemned by the Depression. The 1930 duPont Model G had a 144-inch wheelbase, and used a 322-cid Continental-built side-valve eight with 140 bhp. Most Model G bodies were built by Merrimac; a few were by Waterhouse and Derham. Also in 1930, duPont sold a score of Model Es, which had a smaller supercharged engine. Though duPonts were primarily prestige cars, they did have brief competition experience: A Model G placed highest among all American cars at LeMans in 1929. The Model H, built on a mammoth 146-inch wheelbase, followed in 1931, but only three were built. E. Paul duPont elected to give up the car business in 1932 rather than try to survive on inferior models unworthy of the name. Like Fred Deusenberg, and Fred Moskovics

of Stutz, duPont saw only one way to build a car: He would settle for nothing less than the best. Production of duPonts was strictly limited even in happier days, and it's doubtful more than 100 were built during the 1930s.

DURANT
Durant Motor Company, Muncie, Indiana
William Crapo Durant, the brash and daring founder of General Motors, was shunted out of GM in the late '10s and decided to build a rival empire. Durant Motors, founded in 1921, produced a legion of makes: Star, Flint, Locomobile, Princeton, Rugby, Eagle, and Durant. All but the last were gone by 1930. The best year Billy Durant had was 1923 in which 172,000 cars were completed. In 1930, the Durant line consisted of six models built on a compact 112-inch wheelbase. They used Continental six-cylinder engines with 58 to 70 bhp, mechanical brakes, and had undistinguished styling. By 1931, the line had shrunk to four models selling from $695 to $775. Durant production dropped from 20,900 cars in 1930 to just 7000 in 1931. Volume for 1932 was down to a trickle. A single engine was now offered: the 71-bhp Continental, powering Models 621 and 622. Base price was $700. Durant of America was out of business by early 1932, though its Canadian operation continued selling cars under the Frontenac nameplate through 1933.

ELCAR
Elcar Motor Company, Elkhart, Indiana
This Indiana company never built more than 4000 cars a year, and production was infinitesimal by 1930. But you'd never know it from Elcar's brochure. The 1930 lineup consisted of no fewer than 32 models in four series with three engines and three chassis. The cheapest of these was the 61-bhp Model 75, which had a six-cylinder Lycoming engine and a 117-inch wheelbase. The Elcar 95 and 96 had a Lycoming eight of 90 bhp, and shared a 123-inch wheelbase. The 96 sold for more because of its higher-grade trim. The finest Elcar, and very possibly an overlooked Classic, was the Model 130. This series offered roomy, plush bodies and was priced as high as $2500. Its 130-inch wheelbase mounted a 140-bhp Lycoming-built straight eight, the third-most powerful motor in America at that time. For 1931, Elcar dropped the Model 95 but added the even more luxurious Model 140 on a 135-inch wheelbase. Elcars were finely proportioned, fleet and appealing, but such characteristics doomed the products of many a company in the early '30s. Elcar spent its final days attempting to revive the legendary Mercer, but was out of business by 1932.

GARDNER
Gardner Motor Car Company, St. Louis, Missouri
Russell E. Gardner was reluctant to give up the horse-drawn carriage, and continued building his well known "Banner Buggy" until 1919. Early Gardners were four-cylinder cars; by the '30s, Gardner was using Lyco-

ming sixes and eights. The 1930 Models 136 and 140 ran 70-bhp and 90-bhp sixes, while the 150 had a 126-bhp eight. Wheelbases were 122, 125, and 130 inches, respectively. All Gardners featured hydraulic brakes.

A last-ditch effort to save the company through innovation was the interesting Gardner Front-Drive, which appeared in early 1930. Billed accurately as "the only front-drive car in the $2000 field," it was built impressively low on its 133-inch wheelbase. The lines were clean and classic up to the front end, which was unique. Instead of a flat radiator, the car had a rounded, bisected grille faintly reminiscent of the French Renault. The $2045 Gardner Front-Drive looked impressive, but under the hood was only a peace-loving Lycoming six with just 80 bhp. In its combination of dashing style and anemic engine, the Gardner Front-Drive was not unlike the Cord L-29. And it didn't sell any better than the Cord did, either. After a weak effort to market the same models in 1931, Gardner switched to making hearses and ambulances, and by 1932 was bankrupt.

JORDAN
Jordan Motor Car Company Inc., Cleveland, Ohio
In the 1920s, Edward S. "Ned" Jordan took automotive advertising away from the "straight facts" approach and stirred our imaginations with tales of sunburned gals and blue-blazered guys driving Jordans into fabulous sunsets, seeking the fabled El Dorado. People who bought Jordans fancied themselves as Ned's "Man's Man," or his rangy cowpoke girl from "somewhere west of Laramie," which was exactly as he planned it. Jordan himself was basically a promoter. He built good cars, but he also kept an eye on Wall Street. He was divesting himself of his automotive interests when the crash occurred in October, 1929. Jordan remained president of the firm but the worst of his company's losses were borne by others.

As a make, Jordan went out in style. Its last cars were well put together and impressive to look at. The 1930 range was composed of the Great Line 80 and 90, both eights, using wheelbases of 120 and 125 inches. The engine had 80/85 bhp and the cars would do 100 mph. Sedans were priced at $1495 and $2295, respectively. The 80 came only as a sedan or coupe, but the 90 featured roadsters, convertibles, phaetons, and touring cars as well as closed models. Series 90 roadsters and touring cars used a special 131-inch wheelbase, which was shared with the seven-passenger sedan and limousine.

In addition to a repeat line of 80s and 90s for 1931, Jordan produced its greatest triumph, the Model Z Speedway. This is the only Jordan rated as a Classic by the CCCA. In every way it was magnificent: 145-inch wheelbase, aircraft-inspired instruments including compass and altimeter, running boards shaped like aircraft wing cross-sections, 318-cid Continental straight eight with 125 bhp, and four-speed gearbox. There was a Model Z Sportsman sedan and Ace roadster with custom-built Coburn aluminum bodies and

Minor Makes

both were capable of an easy 100 mph. Each sold for $5500, and we have it on good authority that at least one still exists.

KISSEL
Kissel Motor Company, Hartford, Wisconsin
Like so many others in 1930, Kissel faced a grim future—poor reward for a glorious past. Kissel's speedy Gold Bugs and exotic Silver Specials were all in the past now. So were its many innovations: the double-drop frame, form-fitting seats, all-year bodies, thermostatic engine control, and rubber-cushioned chassis. But there were still some pleasing Kissels to come. The 6-73 had a 117-inch wheelbase and a 70-bhp six. The 125-inch-wheelbase Model 95 had 246 cid and 95 bhp. The Classic-rated 8-126 White Eagle offered wheelbases of up to 139 inches and sold for over $3000; its engine was 298-cid eight with 126 bhp. A Kissel sports roadster was produced in 1930 with the Gold Bug designation—an attempt to invoke a romantic name of the past. Even in its heyday, Kissel had considered 2500 cars a good annual production. There was no point in continuing to offer these finely crafted, almost custom-built, machines in a market one-tenth the size of what it had been. The company was reorganized as Kissel Industries in 1931, and went on to the more prosperous business of building outboard motors.

MERCER
Elcar Motor Company, Elkhart, Indiana
A degree of qualification is needed here. We are not really dealing with a production car, but a stillborn idea: Only two Mercers were built in 1931. Yet it is worth recording that people were *trying* to build them in the Depression. Mercer's Trenton, New Jersey operation had expired in mid 1925, but it continued to supply parts and encourage its devoted owners. One of these, businessman Harry M. Wahl, bought the rights to the Mercer name. Initially, he planned a 137-inch-wheelbase model to be built in Butler, Pennsylvania (where the American Austin eventually started). That didn't work out, so Wahl asked Elcar to build his dream. Elcar was having no luck selling its own models, so it had nothing to lose. The projected 1931 Elcar-built Mercer called for a 322-cid Continental straight eight of 140 bhp. Performance in the 100-mph class was expected. Eight Merrimac bodies were to be offered and the cars would have been priced at $2650 to $4500. The deepening Depression prevented regular production.

PEERLESS
Peerless Motor Car Corp., Cleveland, Ohio
"All that the name implies" was the Peerless slogan, and in earlier years it was just that: one of the finer American cars. Through the early '20s, Peerless ranked with Packard and Pierce-Arrow—the vaunted "Three Ps" of the American industry. When Peerless started to seek higher sales volume in the mid '20s with cheaper cars using proprietary engines, it immediately lost its earlier quality reputation. The 1930 line was composed of Continental sixes and eights, none except the limited-edition Custom Eight priced over $2500. Styling was by Alexis de Sakhnoffsky, and the cars looked good, but Peerless production reached only about 3700 cars in 1930. The 1931 range was reduced to the Standard, Master, and Custom Eight, with 85- and 120-bhp engines. Sedan prices were $1445, $1995, and $2795, respectively. Only the Master and Custom were offered for 1932.

In that year, Peerless made one last-ditch effort to restore its luxury image with a Murphy-bodied V-16. Its aluminum sedan coachwork was svelte and beautiful, and the engine was a huge 450-cid unit with 173 bhp. One can only guess at the price Peerless would have had to ask for this monumental car, but only one Sixteen was completed. The Peerless company happily entered the brewing business after cancelling car operations.

RUXTON
New Era Motors Inc., New York, New York
Here was one of the most interesting and beautiful cars of the 1930s—another great one that died too soon. Its creator was the controversial Archie Andrews, hot-shot promoter and erstwhile Hupp director. The Ruxton used an 85-bhp straight eight to power its ground-hugging front-wheel-drive chassis. The car looked revolutionary with ultra-low hood and fenders, optional Woodlite headlamps (with matching fender-mounted parking lights) and absence of running boards. Less than five feet high, it was incredibly low compared to almost any other car on the market. The Ruxton's announcement, unfortunately timed to coincide almost exactly with the Wall Street crash, did the sales effort little good. Neither did competition from other new front-drive cars like the Cord and Gardner. About 500 were built between June and November, 1930.

STEARNS-KNIGHT
F. B. Stearns Company, Cleveland, Ohio
The Stearns Company was founded in 1899, and built nothing but luxury cars throughout its history. During some years in the '10s, Stearns had the largest engines in the American industry. The firm had begun using Charles Y. Knight's sleeve-valve engines (see Willys) in the mid '10s, and had actually been bought by Willys in a burst of exhuberance in 1925.

The sleeve-valve Stearns-Knight engine displaced 385 cubic inches and developed 127 bhp in this final model year. Eight body styles were offered in the stratospheric price heights of $5000 and up. Most were sedans, though a swank cabriolet roadster was also available. Stearns' three wheelbases were 126, 134, and 145 inches. Styling was formal, upright, and conservative, with a long hood ending in an angular radiator. Stearns continued to supply parts for various defunct makes after halting its own car production in 1930.